Liturgy Documentary Series 2

General Instruction of the Roman Missal

Office of Publishing Services
United States Catholic Conference
Washington, D.C.

First Printing   November 5, 1982
Second Printing   March 8, 1985
Third Printing   June 28, 1988
(Revised to conform with the New Code of
Canon Law)
ISBN 1-55586-852-5

CONTENTS

FOREWORD

In January, 1965, Pope Paul VI established the Consilium, a special commission composed of liturgical experts and bishops from around the world, whose purpose was to implement the principles and decrees contained in the *Constitution on the Sacred Liturgy* of the Second Vatican Council. The monumental task of revising the *Roman Missal* was only one of the many great accomplishments of that Consilium.

That revision appeared in stages, chiefly in the years 1969 and 1970. On April 3, 1969, Pope Paul issued the apostolic constitution *Missale Romanum*, in which he approved the new *Roman Missal* and indicated its new outline. A *General Instruction*, or preface for the book, was to contain the regulations for the celebration of the Eucharist, the structure and elements of the rites, the arrangement and furnishings of sacred spaces, different forms of celebration, and the choice of Mass texts. This instruction would replace the preliminary material in the then current edition of the *Roman Missal*, namely, those sections dealing with general rubrics, the rite to be observed in the celebration and concelebration of Mass, and defects that were to be avoided in the celebration. In addition, the Eucharistic prayer was to be enriched through the inclusion of a greater number of prefaces. New canons would be added. The rites in the *Order of Mass* would be simplified, and in some cases, elements that had suffered injury with the passage of time were to be restored. The *Lectionary* would be revised to include a more representative portion of Sacred Scripture to be read to the people over the course of a set period of years. There were also to be revisions in the Roman Calendar, in ritual Masses and votive Masses.

A few days after the promulgation of the apostolic constitution, the Sacred Congregation of Rites promulgated the typical edition of the *Order of Mass*. Issued at the same time was the first edition of the *General Instruction of the Roman Missal*. Soon after that, on May 25, 1969, the typical edition of the new *Order of Readings* was promulgated. Finally, the Mass formularies contained in the *Sacramentary* were promulgated with the issuing of the first *editio typica* of the *Roman Missal* on March 26, 1970. A second edition of the *General Instruction* was issued together with the *Missal*. It contained some minor changes from the first edition and also included a newly composed Introduction.

In December, 1972, following the suppression of the subdiaconate and minor orders by the motu proprio *Ministeria quaedam*, the Sacred Congregation for Divine Worship issued a third edition of the *General Instruction* that incorporated these ministerial changes. This edition is the one that appears in the American versions of the *Sacramentary*, however, it was not to be the final edition. On March 27, 1975, with the promulgation of the second typical edition of the *Roman Missal*, further changes were made in the Latin text of the *General Instruction*.

The second volume in the *Liturgy Documentary Series* contains the fourth edition (1975) of the *General Instruction* in its English translation prepared by the International Commission on English in the Liturgy. As an added feature, the adaptations to the *Roman Missal* permitted in the *General Instruction* and approved by the National Conference of Catholic Bishops have been included in Appendix 1. And for clarification of various subjects treated in the *General Instruction*, the responses of the Sacred Congregation of Sacraments and Divine Worship to various questions raised in its official publication, *Notitiae*, have been gathered together in Appendix 2.

The *General Instruction of the Roman Missal* is, after the *Constitution on the Sacred Liturgy* itself, the principal liturgical document of the Church dealing with the prayerful celebration of the Eucharist. It is a document of immense importance, especially for priests, deacons, liturgical ministers, and those charged with all aspects of liturgical planning. It is the hope of the Bishops' Committee on the Liturgy that this new edition with its two appendices will be of service to those persons in particular as well as to all the People of God.

Reverend John A. Gurrieri
Executive Director
Secretariat
Bishops' Committee on the Liturgy
National Conference of Catholic Bishops

THE ROMAN MISSAL

Revised by Decree of the Second Vatican Ecumenical Council
and Published by Authority of Pope Paul VI

GENERAL INSTRUCTION OF THE ROMAN MISSAL

English Translation of the Fourth Edition (1975)
prepared by the
International Commission on English in the Liturgy

SACRED CONGREGATION FOR DIVINE WORSHIP

DECREE

The Order of Mass has been established and the texts for the Roman Missal have been approved by Pope Paul VI in the Apostolic Constitution *Missale Romanum*, 3 April 1969.[a] This Congregation for Divine Worship, at the mandate of the Pope, now promulgates and declares to be the *editio typica* this new edition of the Roman Missal prepared in accord with the decrees of Vatican Council II.

As to use of the new Missal, the Latin edition may be put into use as soon as it is published, with the necessary adjustments of saints' days until the revised calendar is put into definitive effect. As to vernacular editions, the conferences of bishops are given the responsibility for their preparation and for setting the effective date for their use, after due confirmation by the Apostolic See.

Anything to the contrary notwithstanding.

From the Sacred Congregation for Divine Worship, 26 March 1970, Holy Thursday.

Benno Card. Gut
prefect

A. Bugnini
secretary

SACRED CONGREGATION FOR DIVINE WORSHIP

DECREE

THE SECOND *EDITIO TYPICA*

Since the Roman Missal must be reprinted, variations and additions have been included in order that this new edition might be in accord with the documents published after the appearance of the first edition in 1970.

In the General Instruction, the marginal numbers are unchanged, but a description of the liturgical functions of acolyte and reader is inserted in place of the paragraphs that formerly dealt with the subdeacon (nos. 142-152).

There is another change of some importance in the section of the Roman Missal that contains the ritual Masses and the Masses for various needs and occasions. Certain formularies have been completed by supplying entrance and communion antiphons.

Texts not found in the first edition have also been added, namely, among the ritual Masses, texts for the Mass of Dedication of a Church and an Altar and for the Mass of Reconciliation, among votive Masses, texts for Masses of Mary, Mother of the Church and of the Most Holy Name of Mary.

Some other, less important changes have been introduced in headings and rubrics so that they may better correspond to the words or expressions occurring in the new liturgical books.

Pope Paul VI has approved this second edition of the Roman Missal by his authority and the Congregation for Divine Worship now issues it and declares it to be the *editio typica*.

It will be the responsibility of the conferences of bishops to introduce into the respective vernacular editions the changes contained in this second edition of the Roman Missal.

Anything to the contrary notwithstanding.

From the Sacred Congregation for Divine Worship, 27 March 1975, Holy Thursday.

James R. Card. Knox
prefect

A. Bugnini
secretary

APOSTOLIC CONSTITUTION

PROMULGATION OF THE ROMAN MISSAL REVISED BY DECREE OF THE SECOND VATICAN ECUMENICAL COUNCIL

PAUL, BISHOP
Servant of the Servants of God
For an Everlasting Memorial

The *Missale Romanum* was promulgated in 1570 by our predecessor St. Pius V, in execution of the decree of the Council of Trent.[1] It has been recognized by all as one of the many admirable results that the Council achieved for the benefit of the entire Church of Christ. For four centuries it provided Latin-rite priests with norms for the celebration of the eucharistic sacrifice; moreover messengers of the Gospel brought this Missal to almost the entire world. Innumerable holy men and women nurtured their spiritual life on its readings from Scripture and on its prayer texts. In large part these prayer texts owed their arrangement to St. Gregory the Great.

A deep interest in fostering the liturgy has become widespread and strong among the Christian people and our predecessor Pius XII has viewed this both as a sign of God's caring will regarding today's people and as a saving movement of the Holy Spirit through his Church.[2] Since the beginning of this liturgical renewal, it has also become clear that the formularies of the Roman Missal had to be revised and enriched. A beginning was made by Pius XII in the restoration of the Easter Vigil and Holy Week services;[3] he thus took the first step toward adapting the Roman Missal to the contemporary mentality.

The Second Vatican Ecumenical Council, in the Constitution *Sacrosanctum Concilium*, laid down the basis for the general revision of the Roman Missal: "Both texts and rites should be drawn up so that they express more clearly the holy things they signify";[4] therefore, "the Order of Mass is to be revised in such a way that the intrinsic nature and purpose of its several parts, as also the connection between them, may be more clearly brought out, and devout, active participation by the faithful more easily achieved."[5] The Council also decreed that "the treasures of the Bible are to be opened up more lavishly, so that a richer share in God's word may be provided for the faithful";[6] and finally that "a new rite for concelebration is to be drawn up and incorporated into the Roman Pontifical and Roman Missal."[7]

No one should think, however, that this revision of the Roman Missal has come out of nowhere. The progress in liturgical studies during the last four centuries has certainly prepared the way. Just after the Council of Trent, the study "of ancient manuscripts in the Vatican library and elsewhere," as St. Pius V attests in the Apostolic Constitution *Quo primum*, helped greatly in the correction of the Roman Missal. Since then, however, other ancient sources have been discovered and published and liturgical formularies of the Eastern Church have been studied. Accordingly many have had the desire for these doctrinal and spiritual riches not to be stored away in the dark, but to be put into use for the enlightenment of the mind of Christians and for the nurture of their spirit.

Now, however, our purpose is to set out at least in broad terms, the new plan of the Roman Missal. We therefore point out, first, that a General Instruction, for use as a preface to the book, gives the new regulations for the celebration of eucharistic sacrifice. These regulations cover the rites to be carried out and the functions of each minister or participant as well as the furnishings and the places needed for divine worship.

It must be acknowledged that the chief innovation in the reform concerns the eucharistic prayer. Although the Roman Rite over the centuries allowed for a multiplicity of different texts in the first part of the prayer (the preface), the second part, called the *Canon actionis*, took on a fixed form during the period of the fourth and fifth centuries. The Eastern liturgies, on the other hand, allowed a degree of variety into the anaphoras themselves. On this point, first of all, the eucharistic prayer has been enriched with a great number of prefaces—drawn from the early tradition of the Roman Church or recently composed—in order that the different facets of the mystery of salvation will stand out more clearly and that there will be more and richer themes of thanksgiving. But besides this, we have decided to add three new canons to the eucharistic prayer. Both for pastoral reasons, however, and for the facilitation of concelebration, we have ordered that the words of the Lord be identical in each form of the canon. Thus in each eucharistic prayer we wish those words to be as follows: over the bread: *Accipite et manducate ex hoc omnes: Hoc est enim Corpus meum, quod pro vobis tradetur;* over the chalice: *Accipite et bibite ex eo omnes: Hic est enim calix Sanguinis mei novi et aeterni testamenti, qui pro vobis et pro multis effundetur in remissionem peccatorum. Hoc facite in meam commemorationem.* The words *Mysterium fidei* have been removed from the context of Christ's own words and are spoken by the priest as an introduction to the faithful's acclamation.

In the Order of Mass the rites have been "simplified, due care being taken to preserve their substance."[8] "Elements that, with the passage of time, came to be duplicated or were added with but little advantage"[9] have been eliminated, especially in the rites for the presentation of the bread and wine, the breaking of the bread, and communion.

Also, "other elements that have suffered injury through accident of history" are restored "to the tradition of the Fathers,"[10] for example, the homily,[11] the general intercessions or prayer of the faithful,[12] and the penitential rite or act of reconciliation with God and the community at the beginning of the Mass, which thus, as is right, regains its proper importance.

According to the decree of the Second Vatican Council, that "a more representative portion of the holy Scriptures be read to the people over the course of a prescribed number of years,"[13] the Sunday readings are arranged in a cycle of three years. In addition, on Sundays and all the major feasts the epistle and gospel are preceded by an Old Testament reading or, at Easter, by readings from Acts. This is meant to provide a fuller exposition of the continuing process of the mystery of salvation, as shown in the words of divine revelation. These broadly selected biblical readings, which set before the faithful on Sundays and holydays the most important part of sacred Scripture, are complemented by other parts of the Bible read on other days.

All this has been planned to arouse among the faithful a greater hunger for the word of God.[14] Under the guidance of the Holy Spirit, this hunger will seem, so to speak, to impel the people of the New Covenant toward the perfect unity of the Church. We are fully confident that under this arrangement both priest and faithful will prepare their minds and hearts more devoutly for the Lord's Supper and that, meditating on the Scriptures, they will be nourished more each day by the words of the Lord. In accord with the teachings of the Second Vatican Council, all will thus regard sacred Scripture as the abiding source of spiritual life, the foundation for Christian instruction, and the core of all theological study.

This reform of the Roman Missal, in addition to the three changes already mentioned (the eucharistic prayer, the Order of Mass, and the readings), has also corrected and considerably modified other of its components: the Proper of Seasons, the Proper of Saints, the Common of Saints, ritual Masses, and votive Masses. In all of these changes, particular care has been taken with the prayers. Their number has been increased, so that the new forms might better correspond to new needs, and the text of older prayers has been restored on the basis of the ancient sources. As a result, each weekday of the principal liturgical seasons, Advent, Christmas, Lent, and Easter, now has its own, distinct prayer.

The text of the *Graduale Romanum* has not been changed as far as the music is concerned. In the interest of their being more readily understood, however, the responsorial psalm (which St. Augustine and St. Leo the Great often mention) as well as the entrance and communion antiphons have been revised for use in Masses that are not sung.

After what we have presented concerning the new Roman Missal, we wish in conclusion to insist on one point in particular and to make it have its effect. When he promulgated the *editio princeps* of the Roman Missal, our predecessor St. Pius V offered it to the people of Christ as the instrument of liturgical unity and the expression of a pure and reverent worship in the Church. Even though, in virtue of the decree of the Second Vatican Council, we have accepted into the new Roman Missal lawful variations and adaptations,[15] our own expectation in no way differs from that of our predecessor. It is that the faithful will receive the new Missal as a help toward witnessing and strengthening their unity with one another; that through the new Missal one and the same prayer in a great diversity of languages will ascend, more fragrant than any incense, to our heavenly Father, through our High Priest, Jesus Christ, in the Holy Spirit.

The effective date for what we have prescribed in this Constitution shall be the First Sunday of Advent of this year, 30 November.[a] We decree that these laws and prescriptions be firm and effective now and in the future, notwithstanding, to the extent necessary, the apostolic constitutions and ordinances issued by our predecessors and other prescriptions, even those deserving particular mention and amendment.

Given at Rome, at Saint Peter's, on Holy Thursday, 3 April 1969, the sixth year of our pontificate.

PAUL PP. VI

[NOTES]

[1]See Ap. Const. *Quo primum*, 14 July 1570.

[2]See Pius XII, Addr. to the participants of the First International Congress on Pastoral Liturgy at Assisi, 22 May 1956: AAS 48 (1956) 712.

[3]See SCR, Decr. *Dominicae Resurrectionis*, 9 Feb. 1951: AAS 43 (1951) 128ff.; Decr. *Maxima redemptionis nostrae mysteria*, 16 Nov. 1955: AAS 47 (1955) 838ff.

[4]SC art. 21.

[5]SC art. 50.

[6]SC art. 51.

[7]SC art. 58.

[8]SC art. 50.

[9]SC art. 50.

[10]SC art. 50.

[11]See SC art. 52.

[12]See SC art. 53.

[13]SC art. 51.

[14]See Amos 8:11.

[15]See SC art. 38-40.

[a] This sentence is left out of the first printing of the Apostolic Constitution *Missale Romanum* as it appeared in the *editio typica* of the *Ordo Missae*

INTRODUCTION

1.   When Christ the Lord was about to celebrate the passover meal with his disciples and institute the sacrifice of his body and blood, he directed them to prepare a large room, arranged for the supper (Lk 22:12). The Church has always regarded this command of Christ as applying to itself when it gives directions about the preparation of the sentiments of the worshipers, the place, rites, and texts for the celebration of the eucharist. The current norms, laid down on the basis of the intent of Vatican Council II, and the new Missal that will be used henceforth in the celebration of Mass by the Church of the Roman Rite, are fresh evidence of the great care, faith, and unchanged love that the Church shows toward the eucharist. They attest as well to its coherent tradition, continuing amid the introduction of some new elements.

A WITNESS TO UNCHANGED FAITH

2.   The sacrificial nature of the Mass was solemnly proclaimed by the Council of Trent in agreement with the whole tradition of the Church.[1] Vatican Council II reaffirmed this teaching in these significant words: "At the Last Supper our Savior instituted the eucharistic sacrifice of his body and blood. He did this in order to perpetuate the sacrifice of the cross throughout the centuries until he should come again and in this way to entrust to his beloved Bride, the Church, a memorial of his death and resurrection."[2]

The Council's teaching is expressed constantly in the formularies of the Mass. This teaching, in the concise words of the Leonine Sacramentary, is that "the work of our redemption is carried out whenever we celebrate the memory of this sacrifice";[3] it is aptly and accurately brought out in the eucharistic prayers. At the anamnesis or memorial, the priest, addressing God in the name of all the people, offers in thanksgiving the holy and living sacrifice: the Church's offering and the Victim whose death has reconciled us with God.[4] The priest also prays that the body and blood of Christ may be a sacrifice acceptable to the Father, bringing salvation to the whole world.[5]

In this new Missal, then, the Church's rule of prayer (lex orandi) corresponds to its constant rulè of faith (lex credendi). This rule of faith instructs us that the sacrifice of the cross and its sacramental renewal in the Mass, which Christ instituted at the Last Supper and commanded his apostles to do in his memory, are one and the same, differing only in the manner of offering and that consequently the Mass is at once a sacrifice of praise and thanksgiving, of reconciliation and expiation.

3.   The celebration of Mass also proclaims the sublime mystery of the Lord's real presence under the eucharistic elements, which Vatican Council II[6] and other documents of the Church's magisterium[7] have reaffirmed in the same sense and as the same teaching that the Council of Trent had proposed as a matter of faith.[8] The Mass does this not only by means of the very words of consecration, by which Christ becomes present through transubstantiation, but also by that spirit and expression of reverence and adoration in which the eucharistic liturgy is carried out. For the same reason the Christian people are invited in Holy Week on Holy Thursday and on the solemnity of Corpus Christi to honor this wonderful sacrament in a special way by their adoration.

4.   Further, because of the priest's more prominent place and office in the rite, its form sheds light on the ministerial priesthood proper to the presbyter, who offers the sacrifice in the person of Christ and presides over the assembly of a holy people. The meaning of his office is declared and detailed in the preface for the chrism Mass on Thursday of Holy Week, the day celebrating the institution of the priesthood. The preface brings out the passing on of the sacerdotal power through the laying on of hands and, by listing its various offices, describes that power. It is the continuation of the power of Christ, High Priest of the New Testament.

5.   In addition, the ministerial priesthood puts into its proper light another reality of which much should be made, namely, the royal priesthood of believers. Through the ministry of presbyters the people's spiritual sacrifice to God is brought to completeness in union with the sacrifice of Christ, our one and only Mediator.[9] For the celebration of the eucharist is the action of the whole Church; in it all should do only, but all of, those parts that belong to them in virtue of their place within the people of God. In this way greater attention will be given to some aspects of the eucharistic celebration that have sometimes been neglected in the course of time. For these people are the people of God, purchased by Christ's blood, gathered together by the Lord, nourished by his word. They are a people called to offer God the prayers of the entire human family, a people giving thanks in Christ for the mystery of salvation by offering his sacrifice. Finally, they are a people growing together into unity by sharing in Christ's body and blood. These people are holy by their origin, but becoming ever more holy by conscious, active, and fruitful participation in the mystery of the eucharist.[10]

A WITNESS TO UNBROKEN TRADITION

6.   In setting forth its decrees for the revision of the Order of Mass, Vatican Council II directed, among other things, that some rites be restored "to the vigor they had in the tradition of the Fathers";[11] this is a quotation from the

16

Apostolic Constitution *Quo primum* of 1570, by which St. Pius V promulgated the Tridentine Missal. The fact that the same words are used in reference to both Roman Missals indicates how both of them, although separated by four centuries, embrace one and the same tradition. And when the more profound elements of this tradition are considered, it becomes clear how remarkably and harmoniously this new Roman Missal improves on the older one.

7.   The older Missal belongs to the difficult period of attacks against Catholic teaching on the sacrificial nature of the Mass, the ministerial priesthood, and the real and permanent presence of Christ under the eucharistic elements. St. Pius V was therefore especially concerned with preserving the relatively recent developments in the Church's tradition, then unjustly being assailed, and introduced only very slight changes into the sacred rites. In fact, the Roman Missal of 1570 differs very little from the first printed edition of 1474, which in turn faithfully follows the Missal used at the time of Pope Innocent III (1198-1216). Manuscripts in the Vatican Library provided some verbal emendations, but they seldom allowed research into "ancient and approved authors" to extend beyond the examination of a few liturgical commentaries of the Middle Ages.

8.   Today, on the other hand, countless studies of scholars have enriched the "tradition of the Fathers" that the revisers of the Missal under St. Pius V followed. After the Gregorian Sacramentary was first published in 1571, many critical editions of other ancient Roman and Ambrosian sacramentaries appeared. Ancient Spanish and Gallican liturgical books also became available, bringing to light many prayers of profound spirituality that had hitherto been unknown.

Traditions dating back to the first centuries before the formation of the Eastern and Western rites are also better known today because so many liturgical documents have been discovered.

The continuing progress in patristic studies has also illumined eucharistic theology through the teachings of such illustrious saints of Christian antiquity as Irenaeus, Ambrose, Cyril of Jerusalem, and John Chrysostom.

9.   The "tradition of the Fathers" does not require merely the preservation of what our immediate predecessors have passed on to us. There must also be profound study and understanding of the Church's entire past and of all the ways in which its single faith has been expressed in the quite diverse human and social forms prevailing in Semitic, Greek, and Latin cultures. This broader view shows us how the Holy Spirit endows the people of God with a marvelous fidelity in preserving the deposit of faith unchanged, even though prayers and rites differ so greatly.

ADAPTATION TO MODERN CONDITIONS

10.   As it bears witness to the Roman Church's rule of prayer (*lex orandi*) and guards the deposit of faith handed down by the later councils, the new Roman Missal in turn marks a major step forward in liturgical tradition.

The Fathers of Vatican Council II in reaffirming the dogmatic statements of the Council of Trent were speaking at a far different time in the world's history. They were able therefore to bring forward proposals and measures of a pastoral nature that could not have even been foreseen four centuries ago.

11.   The Council of Trent recognized the great catechetical value of the celebration of Mass, but was unable to bring out all its consequences for the actual life of the Church. Many were pressing for permission to use the vernacular in celebrating the eucharistic sacrifice, but the Council, judging the conditions of that age, felt bound to answer such a request with a reaffirmation of the Church's traditional teaching. This teaching is that the eucharistic sacrifice is, first and foremost, the action of Christ himself and therefore the manner in which the faithful take part in the Mass does not affect the efficacy belonging to it. The Council thus stated in firm but measured words: "Although the Mass contains much instruction for the faithful, it did not seem expedient to the Fathers that as a general rule it be celebrated in the vernacular."[12] The Council accordingly anathematized anyone maintaining that "the rite of the Roman Church, in which part of the canon and the words of consecration are spoken in a low voice, should be condemned or that the Mass must be celebrated only in the vernacular."[13] Although the Council of Trent on the one hand prohibited the use of the vernacular in the Mass, nevertheless, on the other, it did direct pastors to substitute appropriate catechesis: "Lest Christ's flock go hungry. . .the Council commands pastors and others having the care of souls that either personally or through others they frequently give instructions during Mass, especially on Sundays and holydays, on what is read at Mass and that among their instructions they include some explanation of the mystery of this sacrifice."[14]

12.   Convened in order to adapt the Church to the contemporary requirements of its apostolic task, Vatican Council II examined thoroughly, as had Trent, the pedagogic and pastoral character of the liturgy.[15] Since no Catholic would now deny the lawfulness and efficacy of a sacred rite celebrated in Latin, the Council was able to acknowledge that "the use of the mother tongue frequently may be of great advantage to the people" and gave permission for its use.[16] The enthusiasm in response to this decision was so great that, under the leadership of the bishops and the Apostolic See, it has resulted in the permission for all liturgical celebrations in which the faithful participate to be in the vernacular for the sake of a better comprehension of the mystery being celebrated.

13.   The use of the vernacular in the liturgy may certainly be considered an important means for presenting more clearly the catechesis on the mystery that is part of the celebration itself. Nevertheless, Vatican Council II also ordered the observance of certain directives, prescribed by the Council of Trent but not obeyed everywhere. Among these are the obligatory homily on Sundays and holydays[17] and the permission to interpose some commentary during the sacred rites themselves.[18]

Above all, Vatican Council II strongly endorsed "that more complete form of participation in the Mass by which the faithful, after the priest's communion, receive the Lord's body from the same sacrifice."[19] Thus the Council gave impetus to the fulfillment of the further desire of the Fathers of Trent that for fuller participation in the holy eucharist "the faithful present at each Mass should communicate not only by spiritual desire but also by sacramental communion."[20]

14.   Moved by the same spirit and pastoral concern, Vatican Council II was able to reevaluate the Tridentine norm on communion under both kinds. No one today challenges the doctrinal principles on the completeness of eucharistic communion under the form of bread alone. The Council thus gave permission for the reception of communion under both kinds on some occasions, because this more explicit form of the sacramental sign offers a special means of deepening the understanding of the mystery in which the faithful are taking part.[21]

15.   Thus the Church remains faithful in its responsibility as teacher of truth to guard "things old," that is, the deposit of tradition; at the same time it fulfills another duty, that of examining and prudently bringing forth "things new" (see Mt 13:52).

Accordingly, a part of the new Roman Missal directs the prayer of the Church expressly to the needs of our times. This is above all true of the ritual Masses and the Masses for various needs and occasions, which happily combine the traditional and the contemporary. Thus many expressions, drawn from the Church's most ancient tradition and become familiar through the many editions of the Roman Missal, have remained unchanged. Other expressions, however, have been adapted to today's needs and circumstances and still others—for example, the prayers for the Church, the laity, the sanctification of human work, the community of all peoples, certain needs proper to our era—are completely new compositions, drawing on the thoughts and even the very language of the recent conciliar documents.

The same awareness of the present state of the world also influenced the use of texts from very ancient tradition. It seemed that this cherished treasure would not be harmed if some phrases were changed so that the style of language would be more in accord with the language of modern theology and would faithfully reflect the actual state of the Church's discipline. Thus there have been changes of some expressions bearing on the evaluation and use of the good things of the earth and of allusions to a particular form of outward penance belonging to another age in the history of the Church.

In short, the liturgical norms of the Council of Trent have been completed and improved in many respects by those of Vatican Council II. This Council has brought to realization the efforts of the last four hundred years to move the faithful closer to the sacred liturgy, especially the efforts of recent times and above all the zeal for the liturgy promoted by St. Pius X and his successors.

CHAPTER I
IMPORTANCE AND DIGNITY OF THE EUCHARISTIC CELEBRATION

1.   The celebration of Mass, the action of Christ and the people of God arrayed hierarchically, is for the universal and the local Church as well as for each person the center of the whole Christian life.[1] In the Mass we have the high point of the work that in Christ God accomplishes to sanctify us and the high point of the worship that in adoring God through Christ, his Son, we offer to the Father.[2] During the cycle of the year, moreover, the mysteries of redemption are recalled in the Mass in such a way that they are somehow made present.[3] All other liturgical rites and all the works of the Christian life are linked with the eucharistic celebration, flow from it, and have it as their end.[4]

2.   Therefore, it is of the greatest importance that the celebration of the Mass, the Lord's Supper, be so arranged that the ministers and the faithful who take their own proper part in it may more fully receive its good effects.[5] This is the reason why Christ the Lord instituted the eucharistic sacrifice of his body and blood and entrusted it to the Church, his beloved Bride, as the memorial of his passion and resurrection.[6]

3.   This purpose will best be accomplished if, after due regard for the nature and circumstances of each assembly, the celebration is planned in such a way that it brings about in the faithful a participation in body and spirit that is conscious, active, full, and motivated by faith, hope, and charity. The Church desires this kind of participation, the nature of the celebration demands it, and for the Christian people it is a right and duty they have by reason of their baptism.[7]

4.   The presence and active participation of the people bring out more plainly the ecclesial nature of the celebration.[8] But even when their participation is not possible, the eucharistic celebration still retains its effectiveness and worth because it is the action of Christ and the Church,[9] in which the priest always acts on behalf of the people's salvation.

5.   The celebration of the eucharist, like the entire liturgy, involves the use of outward signs that foster, strengthen, and express faith.[10] There must be

the utmost care therefore to choose and to make wise use of those forms and elements provided by the Church which, in view of the circumstances of the people and the place, will best foster active and full participation and serve the spiritual well-being of the faithful.

6.   The purpose of this Instruction is to give the general guidelines for planning the eucharistic celebration properly and to set forth the rules for arranging the individual forms of celebration.[11] In accord with the Constitution on the Liturgy, each conference of bishops has the power to lay down norms for its own territory that are suited to the traditions and character of peoples, regions, and various communities.[12]

CHAPTER II
STRUCTURE, ELEMENTS, AND PARTS OF THE MASS

I. GENERAL STRUCTURE OF THE MASS

7.   At Mass or the Lord's Supper, the people of God are called together, with a priest presiding and acting in the person of Christ, to celebrate the memorial of the Lord or eucharistic sacrifice.[13] For this reason Christ's promise applies supremely to such a local gathering together of the Church: "Where two or three come together in my name, there am I in their midst" (Mt 18:20). For at the celebration of Mass, which perpetuates the sacrifice of the cross,[14] Christ is really present to the assembly gathered in his name; he is present in the person of the minister, in his own word, and indeed substantially and permanently under the eucharistic elements.[15]

8.   The Mass is made up as it were of the liturgy of the word and the liturgy of the eucharist, two parts so closely connected that they form but one single act of worship.[16] For in the Mass the table of God's word and of Christ's body is laid for the people of God to receive from it instruction and food.[17] There are also certain rites to open and conclude the celebration.

II. DIFFERENT ELEMENTS OF THE MASS
READING AND EXPLAINING THE WORD OF GOD

9.   When the Scriptures are read in the Church, God himself is speaking to his people, and Christ, present in his own word, is proclaiming the Gospel.
    The readings must therefore be listened to by all with reverence; they make up a principal element of the liturgy. In the biblical readings God's word addresses all people of every era and is understandable to them, but a living commentary on the word, that is, the homily, as an integral part of the liturgy, increases the word's effectiveness.[18]

PRAYERS AND OTHER PARTS ASSIGNED TO THE PRIEST

10.   Among the parts assigned to the priest, the eucharistic prayer is preeminent; it is the high point of the entire celebration. Next are the prayers: the

opening prayer or collect, the prayer over the gifts, and the prayer after communion. The priest, presiding over the assembly in the person of Christ, addresses these prayers to God in the name of the entire holy people and all present.[19] Thus there is good reason to call them "the presidential prayers."

11. It is also up to the priest in the exercise of his office of presiding over the assembly to pronounce the instructions and words of introduction and conclusion that are provided in the rites themselves. By their very nature these introductions do not need to be expressed verbatim in the form in which they are given in the Missal; at least in certain cases it will be advisable to adapt them somewhat to the concrete situation of the community.[20] It also belongs to the priest presiding to proclaim the word of God and to give the final blessing. He may give the faithful a very brief introduction to the Mass of the day (before the celebration begins), to the liturgy of the word (before the readings), and to the eucharistic prayer (before the preface); he may also make comments concluding the entire sacred service before the dismissal.

12. The nature of the presidential prayers demands that they be spoken in a loud and clear voice and that everyone present listen with attention.[21] While the priest is reciting them there should be no other prayer and the organ or other instruments should not be played.

13. But the priest does not only pray in the name of the whole community as its president; he also prays at times in his own name that he may exercise his ministry with attention and devotion. Such prayers are said inaudibly.

OTHER TEXTS IN THE CELEBRATION

14. Since by nature the celebration of Mass has the character of being the act of a community,[22] both the dialogues between celebrant and congregation and the acclamations take on special value;[23] they are not simply outward signs of the community's celebration, but the means of greater communion between priest and people.

15. The acclamations and the responses to the priest's greeting and prayers create a degree of the active participation that the gathered faithful must contribute in every form of the Mass, in order to express clearly and to further the entire community's involvement.[24]

16. There are other parts, extremely useful for expressing and encouraging the people's active participation, that are assigned to the whole congregation: the penitential rite, the profession of faith, the general intercessions, and the Lord's Prayer.

17. Finally, of the other texts:
  a. Some constitute an independent rite or act, such as the *Gloria*, the responsorial psalm, the *Alleluia* verse and the verse before the gospel, the *Sanctus*, the memorial acclamation, and the song after communion.

b. Others accompany another rite, such as the songs at the entrance, at the preparation of the gifts, at the breaking of the bread (*Agnus Dei*), and at communion.

VOCAL EXPRESSION OF THE DIFFERENT TEXTS

18.   In texts that are to be delivered in a clear, loud voice, whether by the priest or by the ministers or by all, the tone of voice should correspond to the genre of the text, that is, accordingly as it is a reading, a prayer, an instruction, an acclamation, or a song; the tone should also be suited to the form of celebration and to the solemnity of the gathering. Other criteria are the idiom of different languages and the genius of peoples.

In the rubrics and in the norms that follow, the words *say (dicere)* or *proclaim (proferre)* are to be understood of both singing and speaking, and in accordance with the principles just stated.

IMPORTANCE OF SINGING

19.   The faithful who gather together to await the Lord's coming are instructed by the Apostle Paul to sing psalms, hymns, and inspired songs (see Col 3:16). Song is the sign of the heart's joy (see Acts 2:46). Thus St. Augustine says rightly: "To sing belongs to lovers."[25] There is also the ancient proverb: "One who sings well prays twice."

With due consideration for the culture and ability of each congregation, great importance should be attached to the use of singing at Mass; but it is not always necessary to sing all the texts that are of themselves meant to be sung.

In choosing the parts actually to be sung, however, preference should be given to those that are more significant and especially to those to be sung by the priest or ministers with the congregation responding or by the priest and people together.[26]

Since the faithful from different countries come together ever more frequently, it is desirable that they know how to sing at least some parts of the Ordinary of the Mass in Latin, especially the profession of faith and the Lord's Prayer, set to simple melodies.[27]

MOVEMENTS AND POSTURES

20.   The uniformity in standing, kneeling, or sitting to be observed by all taking part is a sign of the community and the unity of the assembly; it both expresses and fosters the spiritual attitude of those taking part.[28]

21.   For the sake of uniformity in movement and posture, the people should follow the directions given during the celebration by the deacon, the priest, or another minister. Unless other provision is made, at every Mass the people should stand from the beginning of the entrance song or when the priest enters until the end of the opening prayer or collect; for the singing of the *Alleluia* before the gospel; while the gospel is proclaimed; during the profes-

sion of faith and the general intercessions; from the prayer over the gifts to the end of the Mass, except at the places indicated later in this paragraph. They should sit during the readings before the gospel and during the responsorial pslam, for the homily and the presentation of the gifts, and, if this seems helpful, during the period of silence after communion. They should kneel at the consecration unless prevented by the lack of space, the number of people present, or some other good reason.

But it is up to the conference of bishops to adapt the actions and postures described in the Order of the Roman Mass to the customs of the people.[29] But the conference must make sure that such adaptations correspond to the meaning and character of each part of the celebration.

22.   Included among the external actions of the Mass are those of the priest going to the altar, of the faithful presenting the gifts, and their coming forward to receive communion. While the songs proper to these movements are being sung, they should be carried out becomingly in keeping with the norms prescribed for each.

SILENCE

23.   Silence should be observed at the designated times as part of the celebration.[30] Its function depends on the time it occurs in each part of the celebration. Thus at the penitential rite and again after the invitation to pray, all recollect themselves; at the conclusion of a reading or the homily, all meditate briefly on what has been heard; after communion, all praise God in silent prayer.

III. INDIVIDUAL PARTS OF THE MASS
A. Introductory Rites

24.   The parts preceding the liturgy of the word, namely, the entrance song, greeting, penitential rite, *Kyrie*, *Gloria*, and opening prayer or collect, have the character of a beginning, introduction, and preparation.

The purpose of these rites is that the faithful coming together take on the form of a community and prepare themselves to listen to God's word and celebrate the eucharist properly.

ENTRANCE

25.   After the people have assembled, the entrance song begins as the priest and the ministers come in. The purpose of this song is to open the celebration, intensify the unity of the gathered people, lead their thoughts to the mystery of the season or feast, and accompany the procession of priest and ministers.

26.   The entrance song is sung alternately either by the choir and the congregation or by the cantor and the congregation; or it is sung entirely by the congregation or by the choir alone. The antiphon and psalm of the *Graduale Romanum* or *The Simple Gradual* may be used, or another song that is suited

to this part of the Mass, the day, or the seasons and that has a text approved by the conference of bishops.

If there is no singing for the entrance, the antiphon in the Missal is recited either by the faithful, by some of them, or by a reader; otherwise it is recited by the priest after the greeting.

VENERATION OF THE ALTAR AND GREETING OF THE CONGREGATION

27. When the priest and the ministers enter the sanctuary, they reverence the altar. As a sign of veneration, the priest and deacon kiss the altar; when the occasion warrants, the priest may also incense the altar.

28. After the entrance song, the priest and the whole assembly make the sign of the cross. Then through his greeting the priest declares to the assembled community that the Lord is present. This greeting and the congregation's response express the mystery of the gathered Church.

PENITENTIAL RITE

29. After greeting the congregation, the priest or other qualified minister may very briefly introduce the faithful to the Mass of the day. Then the priest invites them to take part in the penitential rite, which the entire community carries out through a communal confession and which the priest's absolution brings to an end.

KYRIE ELEISON

30. Then the *Kyrie* begins, unless it has already been included as part of the penitential rite. Since it is a song by which the faithful praise the Lord and implore his mercy, it is ordinarily prayed by all, that is, alternately by the congregation and the choir or cantor.

As a rule each of the acclamations is said twice, but, because of the idiom of different languages, the music, or other circumstances, it may be said more than twice or a short verse (trope) may be interpolated. If the *Kyrie* is not sung, it is to be recited.

GLORIA

31. The *Gloria* is an ancient hymn in which the Church, assembled in the Holy Spirit, praises and entreats the Father and the Lamb. It is sung by the congregation, or by the congregation alternately with the choir, or by the choir alone. If not sung, it is to be recited either by all together or in alternation.

The *Gloria* is sung or said on Sundays outside Advent and Lent, on solemnities and feasts, and in special, more solemn celebrations.

OPENING PRAYER OR COLLECT

32. Next the priest invites the people to pray and together with him they observe a brief silence so that they may realize they are in God's presence

and may call their petitions to mind. The priest then says the opening prayer, which custom has named the "collect." This expresses the theme of the celebration and the priest's words address a petition to God the Father through Christ in the Holy Spirit.

The people make the prayer their own and give their assent by the acclamation, *Amen.*

In the Mass only one opening prayer is said; this rule applies also to the prayer over the gifts and the prayer after communion.

The opening prayer ends with the longer conclusion, namely:

—if the prayer is directed to the Father: *We ask this (Grant this) through our Lord Jesus Christ, your Son, who lives and reigns with you and the Holy Spirit, one God, for ever and ever;*

—if it is directed to the Father, but the Son is mentioned at the end: *Who lives and reigns with you and the Holy Spirit, one God, for ever and ever;*

—if directed to the Son: *You live and reign with the Father and the Holy Spirit, one God, for ever and ever.*

The prayer over the gifts and the prayer after communion end with the shorter conclusion, namely:

—if the prayer is directed to the Father: *We ask this (Grant this) through Christ our Lord;*

—if it is directed to the Father, but the Son is mentioned at the end: *Who lives and reigns with you for ever and ever;*

—if it is directed to the Son: *You live and reign for ever and ever.*

B. Liturgy of the Word

33.   Readings from Scripture and the chants between the readings form the main part of the liturgy of the word. The homily, profession of faith, and general intercessions or prayer of the faithful expand and complete this part of the Mass. In the readings, explained by the homily, God is speaking to his people,[31] opening up to them the mystery of redemption and salvation, and nourishing their spirit; Christ is present to the faithful through his own word.[32] Through the chants the people make God's word their own and through the profession of faith affirm their adherence to it. Finally, having been fed by this word, they make their petitions in the general intercessions for the needs of the Church and for the salvation of the whole world.

SCRIPTURE READINGS

34.   The readings lay the table of God's word for the faithful and open up the riches of the Bible to them.[33] Since by tradition the reading of the Scriptures is a ministerial, not a presidential function, it is proper that as a rule a deacon or, in his absence, a priest other than the one presiding read the gospel. A reader proclaims the other readings. In the absence of a deacon or another priest, the celebrant reads the gospel.[34]

35. The liturgy itself inculcates the great reverence to be shown toward the reading of the gospel, setting it off from the other readings by special marks of honor. A special minister is appointed to proclaim it and prepares himself by a blessing or prayer. The people, who by their acclamations acknowledge and confess Christ present and speaking to them, stand as they listen to it. Marks of reverence are given to the Book of the Gospels itself.

CHANTS BETWEEN THE READINGS

36. After the first reading comes the responsorial psalm or gradual, an integral part of the liturgy of the word. The psalm as a rule is drawn from the Lectionary because the individual psalm texts are directly connected with the individual readings: the choice of psalm depends therefore on the readings. Nevertheless, in order that the people may be able to join in the responsorial psalm more readily, some texts of responses and psalms have been chosen, according to the different seasons of the year and classes of saints, for optional use, whenever the psalm is sung, in place of the text corresponding to the reading.

The psalmist or cantor of the psalm sings the verses of the psalm at the lectern or other suitable place. The people remain seated and listen, but also as a rule take part by singing the response, except when the psalm is sung straight through without the response.

The psalm when sung may be either the psalm assigned in the Lectionary or the gradual from the *Graduale Romanum* or the responsorial psalm or the psalm with *Alleluia* as the response from *The Simple Gradual* in the form they have in those books.

37. As the season requires, the *Alleluia* or another chant follows the second reading.
   a. The *Alleluia* is sung in every season outside Lent. It is begun either by all present or by the choir or cantor; it may then be repeated. The verses are taken from the Lectionary or the *Graduale*.
   b. The other chant consists of the verse before the gospel or another psalm or tract, as found in the Lectionary or the *Graduale*.

38. When there is only one reading before the gospel:
   a. during a season calling for the *Alleluia*, there is an option to use either the psalm with *Alleluia* as the response, or the responsorial psalm and the *Alleluia* with its verse, or just the psalm, or just the *Alleluia*;
   b. during the season when the *Alleluia* is not allowed, either the responsorial psalm or the verse before the gospel may be used.

39. If the psalm after the reading is not sung, it is to be recited. If not sung, the *Alleluia* or the verse before the gospel may be omitted.

40. Sequences are optional, except on Easter Sunday and Pentecost.

HOMILY

41.   The homily is an integral part of the liturgy and is strongly recommended:[35] it is necessary for the nurturing of the Christian life. It should develop some point of the readings or of another text from the Ordinary or from the Proper of the Mass of the day, and take into account the mystery being celebrated and the needs proper to the listeners.[36]

42.   There must be a homily on Sundays and holydays of obligation at all Masses that are celebrated with a congregation; it may not be omitted without a serious reason. It is recommended on other days, especially on the weekdays of Advent, Lent, and the Easter season, as well as on other feasts and occasions when people come to church in large numbers.[37]
    The homily should ordinarily be given by the priest celebrant.

PROFESSION OF FAITH

43.   The symbol or profession of faith in the celebration of Mass serves as a way for the people to respond and to give their assent to the word of God heard in the readings and through the homily and for them to call to mind the truths of faith before they begin to celebrate the eucharist.

44.   Recitation of the profession of faith by the priest together with the people is obligatory on Sundays and solemnities. It may be said also at special, more solemn celebrations.
    If it is sung, as a rule all are to sing it together or in alternation.

GENERAL INTERCESSIONS

45.   In the general intercessions or prayer of the faithful, the people, exercising their priestly function, intercede for all humanity. It is appropriate that this prayer be included in all Masses celebrated with a congregation, so that petitions will be offered for the Church, for civil authorities, for those oppressed by various needs, for all people, and for the salvation of the world.[38]

46.   As a rule the sequence of intentions is to be:
    a. for the needs of the Church;
    b. for public authorities and the salvation of the world;
    c. for those oppressed by any need;
    d. for the local community.
    In particular celebrations, such as confirmations, marriages, funerals, etc., the series of intercessions may refer more specifically to the occasion.

47.   It belongs to the priest celebrant to direct the general intercessions, by means of a brief introduction to invite the congregation to pray, and after the intercessions to say the concluding prayer. It is desirable that a deacon, cantor, or other person announce the intentions.[39] The whole assembly gives expression to its supplication either by a response said together after each intention or by silent prayer.

C. Liturgy of the Eucharist

48.   At the last supper Christ instituted the sacrifice and paschal meal that make the sacrifice of the cross to be continuously present in the Church, when the priest, representing Christ the Lord, carries out what the Lord did and handed over to his disciples to do in his memory.[40]

Christ took the bread and the cup and gave thanks; he broke the bread and gave it to his disciples, saying: "Take and eat, this is my body." Giving the cup, he said: "Take and drink, this is the cup of my blood. Do this in memory of me." Accordingly, the Church has planned the celebration of the eucharistic liturgy around the parts corresponding to these words and actions of Christ:

1. In the preparation of the gifts, the bread and the wine with water are brought to the altar, that is, the same elements that Christ used.
2. In the eucharistic prayer thanks is given to God for the whole work of salvation and the gifts of bread and wine become the body and blood of Christ.
3. Through the breaking of the one bread the unity of the faithful is expressed and through communion they receive the Lord's body and blood in the same way the apostles received them from Christ's own hands.

PREPARATION OF THE GIFTS

49.   At the beginning of the liturgy of the eucharist the gifts, which will become Christ's body and blood, are brought to the altar.

First the altar, the Lord's table, which is the center of the whole eucharistic liturgy,[41] is prepared: the corporal, purificator, missal, and chalice are placed on it (unless the chalice is prepared at a side table).

The gifts are then brought forward. It is desirable for the faithful to present the bread and wine, which are accepted by the priest or deacon at a convenient place. The gifts are placed on the altar to the accompaniment of the prescribed texts. Even though the faithful no longer, as in the past, bring the bread and wine for the liturgy from their homes, the rite of carrying up the gifts retains the same spiritual value and meaning.

This is also the time to receive money or other gifts for the church or the poor brought by the faithful or collected at the Mass. These are to be put in a suitable place but not on the altar.

50.   The procession bringing the gifts is accompanied by the presentation song, which continues at least until the gifts have been placed on the altar. The rules for this song are the same as those for the entrance song (no. 26). If it is not sung, the presentation antiphon is omitted.

51.   The gifts on the altar and the altar itself may be incensed. This is a symbol of the Church's offering and prayer going up to God. Afterward the deacon or other minister may incense the priest and the people.

52.   The priest then washes his hands as an expression of his desire to be cleansed within.

53.   Once the gifts have been placed on the altar and the accompanying rites completed, the preparation of the gifts comes to an end through the invitation to pray with the priest and the prayer over the gifts, which are a preparation for the eucharistic prayer.

EUCHARISTIC PRAYER

54.   Now the center and summit of the entire celebration begins: the eucharistic prayer, a prayer of thanksgiving and sanctification. The priest invites the people to lift up their hearts to the Lord in prayer and thanks; he unites them with himself in the prayer he addresses in their name to the Father through Jesus Christ. The meaning of the prayer is that the entire congregation joins itself to Christ in acknowledging the great things God has done and in offering the sacrifice.

55.   The chief elements making up the eucharistic prayer are these:
   a. Thanksgiving (expressed especially in the preface): in the name of the entire people of God, the priest praises the Father and gives thanks to him for the whole work of salvation or for some special aspect of it that corresponds to the day, feast, or season.
   b. Acclamation: joining with the angels, the congregation sings or recites the *Sanctus*. This acclamation is an intrinsic part of the eucharistic prayer and all the people join with the priest in singing or reciting it.
   c. Epiclesis: in special invocations the Church calls on God's power and asks that the gifts offered by human hands be consecrated, that is, become Christ's body and blood, and that the victim to be received in communion be the source of salvation for those who will partake.
   d. Institution narrative and consecration: in the words and actions of Christ, that sacrifice is celebrated which he himself instituted at the Last Supper, when, under the appearances of bread and wine, he offered his body and blood, gave them to his apostles to eat and drink, then commanded that they carry on this mystery.
   e. Anamnesis: in fulfillment of the command received from Christ through the apostles, the Church keeps his memorial by recalling especially his passion, resurrection, and ascension.
   f. Offering: in this memorial, the Church—and in particular the Church here and now assembled—offers the spotless victim to the Father in the Holy Spirit. The Church's intention is that the faithful not only offer this victim but also learn to offer themselves and so to surrender themselves, through Christ the Mediator, to an ever more complete union with the Father and with each other, so that at last God may be all in all.[42]
   g. Intercessions: the intercessions make it clear that the eucharist is celebrated in communion with the entire Church of heaven and

earth and that the offering is made for the Church and all its members, living and dead, who are called to share in the salvation and redemption purchased by Christ's body and blood.

h. Final doxology: the praise of God is expressed in the doxology, to which the people's acclamation is an assent and a conclusion.

The eucharistic prayer calls for all to listen in silent reverence, but also to take part through the acclamations for which the rite makes provision.

COMMUNION RITE

56.　Since the eucharistic celebration is the paschal meal, it is right that the faithful who are properly disposed receive the Lord's body and blood as spiritual food as he commanded.[43] This is the purpose of the breaking of bread and the other preparatory rites that lead directly to the communion of the people:

a. Lord's Prayer: this is a petition both for daily food, which for Christians means also the eucharistic bread, and for the forgiveness of sin, so that what is holy may be given to those who are holy. The priest offers the invitation to pray, but all the faithful say the prayer with him; he alone adds the embolism, *Deliver us*, which the people conclude with a doxology. The embolism, developing the last petition of the Lord's Prayer, begs on behalf of the entire community of the faithful deliverance from the power of evil. The invitation, the prayer itself, the embolism, and the people's doxology are sung or are recited aloud.

b. Rite of peace: before they share in the same bread, the faithful implore peace and unity for the Church and for the whole human family and offer some sign of their love for one another.

　　The form the sign of peace should take is left to the conference of bishops to determine, in accord with the culture and customs of the people.

c. Breaking of the bread: in apostolic times this gesture of Christ at the last supper gave the entire eucharistic action its name. This rite is not simply functional, but is a sign that in sharing in the one bread of life which is Christ we who are many are made one body (see 1 Cor 10:17).

d. Commingling: the celebrant drops a part of the host into the chalice.

e. *Agnus Dei:* during the breaking of the bread and the commingling, the *Agnus Dei* is as a rule sung by the choir or cantor with the congregation responding; otherwise it is recited aloud. This invocation may be repeated as often as necessary to accompany the breaking of the bread. The final reprise concludes with the words, *grant us peace.*

f. Personal preparation of the priest: the priest prepares himself by the prayer, said softly, that he may receive Christ's body and blood to good effect. The faithful do the same by silent prayer.

g. The priest then shows the eucharistic bread for communion to the faithful and with them recites the prayer of humility in words from the Gospels.

h. It is most desirable that the faithful receive the Lord's body from hosts consecrated at the same Mass and that, in the instances when it is permitted, they share in the chalice. Then even through the signs communion will stand out more clearly as a sharing in the sacrifice actually being celebrated.[44]

i. During the priest's and the faithful's reception of the sacrament the communion song is sung. Its function is to express outwardly the communicants' union in spirit by means of the unity of their voices, to give evidence of joy of heart, and to make the procession to receive Christ's body more fully an act of community. The song begins when the priest takes communion and continues for as long as seems appropriate while the faithful receive Christ's body. But the communion song should be ended in good time whenever there is to be a hymn after communion.

   An antiphon from the *Graduale Romanum* may also be used, with or without the psalm, or an antiphon with psalm from *The Simple Gradual* or another suitable song approved by the conference of bishops. It is sung by the choir alone or by the choir or cantor with the congregation.

   If there is no singing, the communion antiphon in the Missal is recited either by the people, by some of them, or by a reader. Otherwise the priest himself says it after he has received communion and before he gives communion to the faithful.

j. After communion, the priest and people may spend some time in silent prayer. If desired, a hymn, psalm, or other song of praise may be sung by the entire congregation.

k. In the prayer after communion, the priest petitions for the effects of the mystery just celebrated and by their acclamation, *Amen*, the people make the prayer their own.

D. Concluding Rite

57. The concluding rite consists of:

   a. the priest's greeting and blessing, which on certain days and occasions is expanded and expressed in the prayer over the people or another more solemn formulary;

   b. the dismissal of the assembly, which sends each member back to doing good works, while praising and blessing the Lord.

CHAPTER III
OFFICES AND MINISTRIES IN THE MASS

58.   All in the assembly gathered for Mass have an individual right and duty to contribute their participation in ways differing according to the diversity of their order and liturgical function.[45] Thus in carrying out this function, all, whether ministers or laypersons, should do all and only those parts that belong to them,[46] so that the very arrangement of the celebration itself makes the Church stand out as being formed in a structure of different orders and ministries.

I. OFFICES AND MINISTRIES OF HOLY ORDERS

59.   Every authentic celebration of the eucharist is directed by the bishop, either in person or through the presbyters, who are his helpers.[47]

Whenever he is present at a Mass with a congregation, it is fitting that the bishop himself preside over the assembly and associate the presbyters with himself in the celebration, if possible by concelebrating with them.

This is done not to add external solemnity, but to express in a clearer light the mystery of the Church, which is the sacrament of unity.[48]

Even if the bishop is not the celebrant of the eucharist but assigns someone else, he should preside over the liturgy of the word and give the blessing at the end of Mass.

60.   Within the community of believers, the presbyter is another who possesses the power of orders to offer sacrifice in the person of Christ.[49] He therefore presides over the assembly and leads its prayer, proclaims the message of salvation, joins the people to himself in offering the sacrifice to the Father through Christ in the Spirit, gives them the bread of eternal life, and shares in it with them. At the eucharist he should, then, serve God and the people with dignity and humility; by his bearing and by the way he recites the words of the liturgy he should communicate to the faithful a sense of the living presence of Christ.

61.   Among ministers, the deacon, whose order has been held in high honor since the early Church, has first place. At Mass he has his own functions: he proclaims the gospel, sometimes preaches God's word, leads the general

intercessions, assists the priest, gives communion to the people (in particular, ministering the chalice), and sometimes gives directions regarding the assembly's moving, standing, kneeling, or sitting.

II. OFFICE AND FUNCTION OF THE PEOPLE OF GOD

62. In the celebration of Mass the faithful are a holy people, a people God has made his own, a royal priesthood: they give thanks to the Father and offer the victim not only through the hands of the priest but also together with him and learn to offer themselves.[50] They should endeavor to make this clear by their deep sense of reverence for God and their charity toward all who share with them in the celebration.

They therefore are to shun any appearance of individualism or division, keeping before their mind that they have the one Father in heaven and therefore are all brothers and sisters to each other.

They should become one body, whether by hearing the word of God, or joining in prayers and song, or above all by offering the sacrifice together and sharing together in the Lord's table. There is a beautiful expression of this unity when the faithful maintain uniformity in their actions and in standing, sitting, or kneeling.

The faithful should serve the people of God willingly when asked to perform some particular ministry in the celebration.

63. The *schola cantorum* or choir exercises its own liturgical function within the assembly. Its task is to ensure that the parts proper to it, in keeping with the different types of chants, are carried out becomingly and to encourage active participation of the people in the singing.[51] What is said about the choir applies in a similar way to other musicians, especially the organist.

64. There should be a cantor or a choir director to lead and sustain the people in the singing. When in fact there is no choir, it is up to the cantor to lead the various songs, and the people take part in the way proper to them.[52]

III. SPECIAL MINISTRIES

65. The acolyte is instituted to serve at the altar and to assist the priest and deacon. In particular it is for him to prepare the altar and the vessels and, as a special minister of the eucharist, to give communion to the faithful.

66. The reader is instituted to proclaim the readings from Scripture, with the exception of the gospel. He may also announce the intentions for the general intercessions and, in the absence of the psalmist, sing or read the psalm between the readings.

The reader has his own proper function in the eucharistic celebration and should exercise this even though ministers of a higher rank may be present.

Those who exercise the ministry of reader, even if they have not received institution, must be truly qualified and carefully prepared in order that the faithful will develop a warm and lively love for Scripture[53] from listening to the reading of the sacred texts.

67.   The cantor of the psalm is to sing the psalm or other biblical song that comes between the readings. To fulfill their function correctly, these cantors should possess singing talent and an aptitude for correct pronunciation and diction.

68.   As for other ministers, some perform different functions inside the sanctuary, others outside.

The first kind include those deputed as special ministers to administer communion[54] and those who carry the missal, the cross, candles, the bread, wine, water, and the thurible.

The second kind include:
   a. The commentator. This minister provides explanations and commentaries with the purpose of introducing the faithful to the celebration and preparing them to understand it better. The commentator's remarks must be meticulously prepared and marked by a simple brevity.

   In performing this function the commentator stands in a convenient place visible to the faithful, but it is preferable that this not be at the lectern where the Scriptures are read.
   b. Those who, in some places, meet the people at the church entrance, seat them, and direct processions.
   c. Those who take up the collection.

69.   Especially in larger churches and communities, a person should be assigned responsibility for planning the services properly and for their being carried out by the ministers with decorum, order, and devotion.

70.   Laymen, even if they have not received institution as ministers, may perform all the functions below those reserved to deacons. At the discretion of the rector of the church, women may be appointed to ministries that are performed outside the sanctuary.

The conference of bishops may permit qualified women to proclaim the readings before the gospel and to announce the intentions of the general intercessions. The conference may also more precisely designate a suitable place for a woman to proclaim the word of God in the liturgical assembly.[55]

71.   If there are several persons present who are empowered to exercise the same ministry, there is no objection to their being assigned different parts to perform. For example, one deacon may take the sung parts, another assist at the altar; if there are several readings, it is better to distribute them among a number of readers. The same applies for the other ministries.

72.   If only one minister is present at a Mass with a congregation, he may carry out several different functions.

73.   All concerned should work together in the effective preparation of each liturgical celebration as to its rites, pastoral aspects, and music. They should work under the direction of the rector of the church and should consult the faithful.

CHAPTER IV
THE DIFFERENT FORMS OF CELEBRATION

74.   In the local Church, first place should be given, because of its meaning, to the Mass at which the bishop presides surrounded by the college of presbyters and the ministers[56] and in which the people take full and active part. For this Mass is the preeminent expression of the Church.

75.   Great importance should be attached to a Mass celebrated by any community, but especially by the parish community, inasmuch as it represents the universal Church gathered at a given time and place. This is particularly true of the community's celebration of the Lord's Day.[57]

76.   Of those Masses celebrated by some communities, the conventual Mass, which is a part of the daily office, or the "community" Mass have particular significance. Although such Masses do not have a special form of celebration, it is most proper that they be celebrated with singing, with the full participation of all community members, whether religious or canons. In these Masses, therefore, individuals should exercise the function proper to the order or ministry they have received. All the priests who are not bound to celebrate individually for the pastoral benefit of the faithful should thus concelebrate at the conventual or community Mass, if possible. Further, all priests belonging to the community who are obliged to celebrate individually for the pastoral benefit of the faithful may also on the same day concelebrate at the conventual or community Mass.[58]

I. MASS WITH A CONGREGATION

77.   Mass with a congregation means a Mass celebrated with the people taking part. As far as possible, and especially on Sundays and holydays of obligation, this Mass should be celebrated with song and with a suitable number of ministers.[59] But it may be celebrated without music and with only one minister.

78.   It is desirable that as a rule an acolyte, a reader, and a cantor assist the priest celebrant; this form of celebration will hereafter be referred to as the "basic" or "typical" form. But the rite to be described also allows for a greater number of ministers.

A deacon may exercise his office in any of the forms of celebration.

ARTICLES TO BE PREPARED

79.   The altar is to be covered with at least one cloth. On or near the altar there are to be candlesticks with lighted candles, at least two but even four, six, or, if the bishop of the diocese celebrates, seven. There is also to be a cross on or near the altar. The candles and cross may be carried in the entrance procession. The Book of the Gospels, if distinct from the book of other readings, may be placed on the altar, unless it is carried in the entrance procession.

80.   The following are also to be prepared:
   a. next to the priest's chair: the missal and, as may be useful, a book with the chants;
   b. at the lectern: the lectionary;
   c. on a side table: the chalice, corporal, purificator, and, if useful, a pall; a paten and ciboria, if needed, with the bread for the communion of the ministers and the people, together with cruets containing wine and water, unless all of these are brought in by the faithful at the presentation of the gifts; communion plate for the communion of the faithful; the requisites for the washing of hands. The chalice should be covered with a veil, which may always be white.

81.   In the sacristy the vestments for the priest and ministers are to be prepared according to the various forms of celebration:
   a. for the priest: alb, stole, and chasuble;
   b. for the deacon: alb, stole, and dalmatic; the last may be omitted either out of necessity or for less solemnity;
   c. for the other ministers: albs or other lawfully approved vestments.
   All who wear an alb should use a cincture and an amice, unless other provision is made.

A. Basic Form of Celebration

INTRODUCTORY RITES

82.   Once the congregation has gathered, the priest and the ministers, clad in their vestments, go to the altar in this order:
   a. a server with a lighted censer, if incense is used;
   b. the servers, who, according to the occasion, carry lighted candles, and between them the crossbearer, if the cross is to be carried;
   c. acolytes and other ministers;
   d. a reader, who may carry the Book of the Gospels;
   e. the priest who is to celebrate the Mass.
   If incense is used, the priest puts some in the censer before the procession begins.

83.   During the procession to the altar the entrance song is sung (see nos. 25-26).

84.   On reaching the altar the priest and ministers make the proper reverence, that is, a low bow or, if there is a tabernacle containing the blessed sacrament, a genuflection.

If the cross has been carried in the procession, it is placed near the altar or at some other convenient place; the candles carried by the servers are placed near the altar or on a side table; the Book of the Gospels is placed on the altar.

85.   The priest goes up to the altar and kisses it. If incense is used, he incenses the altar while circling it.

86.   The priest then goes to the chair. After the entrance song, and with all standing, the priest and the faithful make the sign of the cross. The priest says: *In the name of the Father, and of the Son, and of the Holy Spirit;* the people answer: *Amen.*

Then, facing the people and with hands outstretched, the priest greets all present, using one of the formularies indicated. He or some other qualified minister may give the faithful a very brief introduction to the Mass of the day.

87.   After the penitential rite, the *Kyrie* and *Gloria* are said, in keeping with the rubrics (nos. 30-31). Either the priest or the cantors or even everyone together may begin the *Gloria.*

88.   With his hands joined, the priest then invites the people to pray, saying: *Let us pray.* All pray silently with the priest for a while. Then the priest with hands outstretched says the opening prayer, at the end of which the people respond: *Amen.*

LITURGY OF THE WORD

89.   After the opening prayer, the reader goes to the lectern for the first reading. All sit and listen and make the acclamation at the end.

90.   After the reading, the psalmist or cantor of the psalm, or even the reader, sings or recites the psalm and the congregation sings or recites the response (see no. 36).

91.   Then, if there is a second reading before the gospel, the reader reads it at the lectern as before. All sit and listen and make the acclamation at the end.

92.   The *Alleluia* or other chant, according to the season, follows (see nos. 37-39).

93.   During the singing of the *Alleluia* or other chant, if incense is being used, the priest puts some into the censer. Then with hands joined he bows before the altar and says softly the prayer, *Almighty God, cleanse my heart.*

94.   If the Book of the Gospels is on the altar, he takes it and goes to the lectern, the servers, who may carry the censer and candles, walking ahead of him.

95.   At the lectern the priest opens the book and says: *The Lord be with you.* Then he says: *A reading from. . .*, making the sign of the cross with his thumb on the book and on his forehead, mouth, and breast. If incense is used, he then incenses the book. After the acclamation of the people, he proclaims the gospel and at the end kisses the book, saying softly: *May the words of the gospel wipe away our sins.* After the reading the people make the acclamation customary to the region.

96.   If no reader is present, the priest himself proclaims all the readings at the lectern and there also, if necessary, the chants between the readings. If incense is used, he puts some into the censer at the lectern and then, bowing, says the prayer, *Almighty God, cleanse my heart.*

97.   The homily is given at the chair or at the lectern.

98.   The profession of faith is said by the priest together with the people (see no. 44). At the words, *by the power of the Holy Spirit*, etc., all bow; on the solemnities of the Annunciation and Christmas all kneel.

99.   Next, with the people taking their proper part, follow the general intercessions (prayer of the faithful), which the priest directs from his chair or at the lectern (see nos. 45-47).

LITURGY OF THE EUCHARIST

100.   After the general intercessions, the presentation song begins (see no. 50). The servers place the corporal, purificator, chalice, and missal on the altar.

101.   It is fitting for the faithful's participation to be expressed by their presenting both the bread and wine for the celebration of the eucharist and other gifts to meet the needs of the church and of the poor.

The faithful's offerings are received by the priest, assisted by the ministers, and put in a suitable place; the bread and wine for the eucharist are taken to the altar.

102.   At the altar the priest receives the paten with the bread from a minister. With both hands he holds it slightly raised above the altar and says the accompanying prayer. Then he places the paten with the bread on the corporal.

103.   Next, as a minister presents the cruets, the priest stands at the side of the altar and pours wine and a little water into the chalice, saying the accompanying prayer softly. He returns to the middle of the altar, takes the chalice, raises it a little with both hands, and says the appointed prayer. Then he places the chalice on the corporal and may cover it with a pall.

104. The priest bows and says softly the prayer, *Lord God, we ask you to receive.*

105. If incense is used, he incenses the gifts and the altar. A minister incenses the priest and the congregation.

106. After the prayer, *Lord God, we ask you to receive,* or after the incensation, the priest washes his hands at the side of the altar and softly says the prescribed prayer as a minister pours the water.

107. The priest returns to the center and, facing the people and extending then joining his hands, pronounces the invitation: *Pray, brothers and sisters.* After the people's response, he says the prayer over the gifts with hands outstretched. At the end the people make the acclamation: *Amen.*

108. The priest then begins the eucharistic prayer. With hands outstretched, he says: *The Lord be with you.* As he says: *Lift up your hearts,* he raises his hands; with hands outstretched, he adds: *Let us give thanks to the Lord our God.* When the people have answered: *It is right to give him thanks and praise,* the priest continues the preface. At its conclusion, he joins his hands and sings or says aloud with the ministers and people the *Sanctus-Benedictus* (see no. 55 b).

109. The priest continues the eucharistic prayer according to the rubrics that are given for each of them. If the priest celebrant is a bishop, after the words *N. our Pope* or the equivalent, he adds: *and for me your unworthy servant.* The local Ordinary must be mentioned in this way: *N. our Bishop* (or *Vicar, Prelate, Prefect, Abbot*). Coadjutor and auxiliary bishops may be mentioned in the eucharistic prayer. When several are named, this is done with the collective formula, *N. our Bishop and his assistant bishops.*[60] All these phrases should be modified grammatically to fit each of the eucharistic prayers.

A little before the consecration, the server may ring a bell as a signal to the faithful. Depending on local custom, he also rings the bell at the showing of both the host and the chalice.

110. After the doxology at the end of the eucharistic prayer, the priest, with hands joined, says the introduction to the Lord's Prayer. With hands outstretched he then sings or says this prayer with the people.

111. After the Lord's Prayer, the priest alone, with hands outstretched, says the embolism, *Deliver us.* At the end the congregation makes the acclamation, *For the kingdom.*

112. Then the priest says aloud the prayer, *Lord Jesus Christ.* After this prayer, extending then joining his hands, he gives the greeting of peace: *The peace of the Lord be with you always.* The people answer: *And also with you.* Then the priest may add: *Let us offer each other a sign of peace.* All exchange some sign of peace and love, according to local custom. The priest may give the sign of peace to the ministers.

113. The priest then takes the eucharistic bread and breaks it over the paten. He places a small piece in the chalice, saying softly: *May this mingling.* Meanwhile the *Agnus Dei* is sung or recited by the choir and congregation (see no. 56 e).

114. Then the priest says softly the prayer, *Lord Jesus Christ, Son of the living God,* or *Lord Jesus Christ, with faith in your love and mercy.*

115. After the prayer the priest genuflects, takes the eucharistic bread, and, holding it slightly above the paten while facing the people, says: *This is the Lamb of God.* With the people he adds, once only: *Lord, I am not worthy to receive you.*

116. Next, facing the altar, the priest says softly: *May the body of Christ bring me to everlasting life* and reverently consumes the body of Christ. Then he takes the chalice, saying: *May the blood of Christ bring me to everlasting life,* and reverently drinks the blood of Christ.

117. He then takes the paten or a ciborium and goes to the communicants. If communion is given only under the form of bread, he raises the eucharistic bread slightly and shows it to each one, saying: *The body of Christ.* The communicants reply: *Amen* and, holding the communion plate under their chin, receive the sacrament.

118. For communion under both kinds, the rite described in nos. 240-252 is followed.

119. The communion song is begun while the priest is receiving the sacrament (see no. 56 i).

120. After communion the priest returns to the altar and collects any remaining particles. Then, standing at the side of the altar or at a side table, he purifies the paten or ciborium over the chalice, then purifies the chalice, saying quietly: *Lord, may I receive these gifts,* etc., and dries it with a purificator. If this is done at the altar, the vessels are taken to a side table by a minister. It is also permitted, especially if there are several vessels to be purified, to leave them, properly covered and on a corporal, either at the altar or at a side table and to purify them after Mass when the people have left.

121. Afterward the priest may return to the chair. A period of silence may now be observed, or a hymn of praise or a psalm may be sung (see no. 56 j).

122. Then, standing at the altar or at the chair and facing the people, the priest says, with hands outstretched: *Let us pray.* There may be a brief period of silence, unless this has been already observed immediately after communion. He recites the prayer after communion, at the end of which the people make the response: *Amen.*

CONCLUDING RITES

123. If there are any brief announcements, they may be made at this time.

124. Then the priest, with hands outstretched, greets the people: *The Lord be with you.* They answer: *And also with you.* The priest immediately adds: *May almighty God bless you* and, as he blesses with the sign of the cross, continues: *the Father, and the Son, and the Holy Spirit.* All answer: *Amen.* On certain days and occasions another, more solemn form of blessing or the prayer over the people precedes this form of blessing as the rubrics direct.

Immediately after the blessing, with hands joined, the priest adds: *Go in the peace of Christ,* or: *Go in peace to love and serve the Lord,* or: *The Mass is ended, go in peace,* and the people answer: *Thanks be to God.*

125. As a rule, the priest then kisses the altar, makes the proper reverence with the ministers, and leaves.

126. If another liturgical service follows the Mass, the concluding rites (greeting, blessing, and dismissal) are omitted.

B. Functions of the Deacon

127. When there is a deacon present to exercise his ministry, the norms in the preceding section apply, with the following exceptions.

In general the deacon: a. assists the priest and walks at his side; b. at the altar, assists with the chalice or the book; c. if there is no other minister present, carries out other ministerial functions as required.

INTRODUCTORY RITES

128. Vested and carrying the Book of the Gospels, the deacon precedes the priest on the way to the altar or else walks at the priest's side.

129. With the priest he makes the proper reverence and goes up to the altar. After placing the Book of the Gospels on it, along with the priest he kisses the altar. If incense is used, he assists the priest in putting some in the censer and in incensing the altar.

130. After the incensing, he goes to the chair with the priest, sits next to him, and assists him as required.

LITURGY OF THE WORD

131. If incense is used, the deacon assists the priest when he puts incense in the censer during the singing of the *Alleluia* or other chant. Then he bows before the priest and asks for the blessing, saying in a low voice: *Father, give me your blessing.* The priest blesses him: *The Lord be in your heart.* The deacon answers: *Amen.* If the Book of the Gospels is on the altar, he takes it and goes to the lectern; the servers, if there are any, precede, carrying candles and the censer when used. At the lectern the deacon greets the people, incenses the book, and proclaims the gospel. After the reading, he kisses the book, saying softly: *May the words of the gospel wipe away our sins,* and returns to the priest. If there is no homily or profession of faith, he may remain at the lectern for the general intercessions, but the servers leave.

132. After the priest introduces the general intercessions, the deacon announces the intentions at the lectern or other suitable place.

LITURGY OF THE EUCHARIST

133. At the presentation of the gifts, while the priest remains at the chair, the deacon prepares the altar, assisted by other ministers, but the care of the sacred vessels belongs to the deacon. He assists the priest in receiving the people's gifts. Next, he hands the priest the paten with the bread to be consecrated, pours wine and a little water into the chalice, saying softly the *Through the mystery of this water and wine*, then passes the chalice to the priest. (He may also prepare the chalice and pour the wine and water at a side table.) If incense is used, the deacon assists the priest with the incensing of the gifts and the altar; afterward he, or another minister, incenses the priest and the people.

134. During the eucharistic prayer, the deacon stands near but slightly behind the priest, so that when necessary he may assist the priest with the chalice or the missal.

135. At the final doxology of the eucharistic prayer, the deacon stands next to the priest, holding up the chalice as the priest raises the paten with the eucharistic bread, until the people have said the acclamation: *Amen*.

136. After the priest has said the prayer for peace and the greeting: *The peace of the Lord be with you always*, and the people have made the response: *And also with you*, the deacon may invite all to exchange the sign of peace, saying: *Let us offer each other the sign of peace*. He himself receives the sign of peace from the priest and may offer it to other ministers near him.

137. After the priest's communion, the deacon receives under both kinds and then assists the priest in giving communion to the people. But if communion is given under both kinds, the deacon ministers the chalice to the communicants and is the last to drink from it.

138. After communion, the deacon returns to the altar with the priest and collects any remaining fragments. He then takes the chalice and other vessels to the side table, where he purifies them and arranges them in the usual way; the priest returns to the chair. But it is permissable to leave the vessels to be purified, properly covered and on a corporal, at a side table and to purify them after Mass, when the people have left.

CONCLUDING RITE

139. Following the prayer after communion, if there are any brief announcements, the deacon may make them, unless the priest prefers to do so himself.

140. After the priest's blessing, the deacon dismisses the people, saying: *Go in the peace of Christ*, or: *Go in peace to love and serve the Lord*, or: *The Mass is ended, go in peace*.

141. Along with the priest, the deacon kisses the altar, makes the proper reverence, and leaves in the manner followed for the entrance procession.

C. Functions of the Acolyte

142. The acolyte may have functions of various kinds and several may occur at the same time. It is therefore desirable that these functions be suitably distributed among several acolytes. But if there is only a single acolyte present, he should perform the more important functions and the rest are distributed among other ministers.

INTRODUCTORY RITES

143. In the procession to the altar the acolyte may carry the cross, walking between two servers with lighted candles. When he reaches the altar, he places the cross near it and takes his own place in the sanctuary.

144. Throughout the celebration it belongs to the acolyte to go to the priest or the deacon, whenever necessary, in order to present the book to them and to assist them in any other way required. Thus it is appropriate that, if possible, he have a place from which he can conveniently carry out his ministry both at the chair and at the altar.

LITURGY OF THE EUCHARIST

145. After the general intercessions, when no deacon is present, the acolyte places the corporal, purificator, chalice, and missal on the altar, while the priest remains at the chair. Then, if necessary, the acolyte assists the priest in receiving the gifts of the people and he may bring the bread and wine to the altar and present them to the priest. If incense is used, the acolyte gives the censer to the priest and assists him in incensing the gifts and the altar.

146. The acolyte may assist the priest as a special minister in giving communion to the people.[61] If communion is given under both kinds, the acolyte ministers the chalice to the communicants or he holds the chalice when communion is given by intinction.

147. After communion, the acolyte helps the priest or deacon to purify and arrange the vessels. If no deacon is present, the acolyte takes the vessels to the side table, where he purifies and arranges them.

D. Functions of the Reader

INTRODUCTORY RITES

148. In the procession to the altar, when no deacon is present, the reader may carry the Book of the Gospels. In that case he walks in front of the priest; otherwise he walks with the other ministers.

149. Upon reaching the altar, the reader makes the proper reverence along with the priest, goes up to the altar, and places the Book of the Gospels on it. Then he takes his place in the sanctuary with the other ministers.

150. At the lectern the reader proclaims the readings that precede the gospel. If there is no cantor of the psalm, he may also sing or recite the responsorial psalm after the first reading.

151. After the priest gives the introduction to the general intercessions, the reader may announce the intentions when no deacon is present.

152. If there is no entrance song or communion song and the antiphons in the Missal are not said by the faithful, the reader recites them at the proper time.

II. CONCELEBRATED MASSES
INTRODUCTION

153. Concelebration effectively brings out the unity of the priesthood, of the sacrifice, and of the whole people of God. The rite itself prescribes concelebration at the ordination of bishops and of priests and at the chrism Mass.
　　Unless the good of the faithful requires or suggests otherwise, concelebration is also recommended at:
　　a. the evening Mass on Holy Thursday;
　　b. the Mass for councils, meetings of bishops, and synods;
　　c. the Mass for the blessing of an abbot;
　　d. the conventual Mass and the principal Mass in churches and oratories;
　　e. the Mass for any kind of meeting of priests, either secular or religious.[62]

154. Where there is a large number of priests, the authorized superior may permit concelebration several times on the same day, but either at different times or in different places.[63]

155. The right to regulate, in accord with the law, the discipline for concelebration in his diocese, even in churches and oratories of exempt religious, belongs to the bishop.[64]

156. No one is ever to be admitted into a concelebration once Mass has already begun.[65]

157. A concelebration in which the priests of any diocese concelebrate with their own bishop, especially at the chrism Mass on Holy Thursday and on the occasion of a synod or pastoral visitation, is to be held in high regard. Concelebration is likewise recommended whenever priests gather together with their bishop during a retreat or at any other meeting. That sign of the

unity of the priesthood and of the Church itself which marks every concelebration stands out even more clearly in the instances mentioned.[66]

158. For a particular reason, having to do either with the meaning of the rite or of the liturgical feast, to celebrate or concelebrate more than once on the same day is permitted as follows:

    a. One who has celebrated or concelebrated the chrism Mass on Holy Thursday may also celebrate or concelebrate the evening Mass.

    b. One who has celebrated or concelebrated the Mass of the Easter Vigil may celebrate or concelebrate the second Mass of Easter.

    c. All priests may celebrate or concelebrate the three Masses of Christmas, provided the Masses are at their proper times of day.

    d. One who concelebrates with the bishop or his delegate at a synod or pastoral visitation, or concelebrates on the occasion of a meeting of priests, may celebrate another Mass for the benefit of the people.[67] This holds also, in analogous circumstances, for gatherings of religious.

159. The structure of a concelebrated Mass, whatever its form, follows the norms for an individual celebration, except for the points prescribed or changed in the next section.

160. If neither a deacon nor other ministers assist in a concelebrated Mass, their functions are carried out by the concelebrants.

INTRODUCTORY RITES

161. In the sacristy or other suitable place, the concelebrants put on the vestments usual for individual celebrants. For a good reason, however, as when there are more concelebrants than vestments, the concelebrants may omit the chasuble and simply wear the stole over the alb; but the principal celebrant always wears the chasuble.

162. When everything is ready, there is the usual procession through the church to the altar. The concelebrating priests go ahead of the principal celebrant.

163. On reaching the altar, the concelebrants and the celebrant make the prescribed reverence, kiss the altar, then go to their chairs. When incense is used, the principal celebrant incenses the altar, then goes to the chair.

LITURGY OF THE WORD

164. During the liturgy of the word, the concelebrants remain at their places, sitting or standing as the principal celebrant does.

165. As a rule the principal celebrant or one of the concelebrants gives the homily.

LITURGY OF THE EUCHARIST

166. The rites for the preparation of the gifts are carried out by the principal celebrant; the other concelebrants remain at their places.

167. At the end of the preparation of the gifts, the concelebrants come near the altar and stand around it in such a way that they do not interfere with the actions of the rite and that the people have a clear view. They should not be in the deacon's way when he has to go to the altar in the performance of his ministry.

MANNER OF RECITING THE EUCHARISTIC PRAYER

168. The preface is said by the principal celebrant alone; the *Sanctus* is sung or recited by all the concelebrants with the congregation and the choir.

169. After the *Sanctus*, the concelebrants continue the eucharistic prayer in the way to be described. Unless otherwise indicated, only the principal celebrant makes the gestures.

170. The parts said by all the concelebrants together are to be recited in such a way that the concelebrants say them in a softer voice and the prinicpal celebrant's voice stands out clearly. In this way the congregation should be able to hear the text without difficulty.

A. Eucharistic Prayer I, the Roman Canon

171. The prayer, *We come to you, Father*, is said by the principal celebrant alone, with hands outstretched.

172. The intercessions, *Remember, Lord, your people* and *In union with the whole Church*, may be assigned to one of the concelebrants; he alone says these prayers, with hands outstretched and aloud.

173. The prayer, *Father, accept this offering*, is said by the principal celebrant alone, with hands outstretched.

174. From *Bless and approve our offering* to *Almighty God, we pray* inclusive, all the concelebrants recite everything together in this manner:
   a. They say *Bless and approve our offering* with hands outstretched toward the offerings.
   b. They say *The day before he suffered* and *When supper was ended* with hands joined.
   c. While saying the words of the Lord, each extends his right hand toward the bread and toward the chalice, if this seems appropriate; they look at the eucharistic bread and chalice as these are shown and afterward bow low.
   d. They say *Father, we celebrate the memory of Christ* and *Look with favor* with hands outstretched.
   e. From *Almighty God, we pray* to *the sacred body and blood of your Son* inclusive, they bow with hands joined; then they stand upright and cross themselves at the words, *let us be filled*.

175. The intercessions, *Remember, Lord, those who have died* and *For ourselves, too*, may be assigned to one of the concelebrants; he alone says these prayers, with hands outstretched and aloud.

176. At the words, *Though we are sinners,* all the concelebrants strike their breast.

177. The prayer, *Through Christ our Lord you give us all these gifts,* is said by the principal celebrant alone.

178. In this eucharistic prayer the parts from *Bless and approve our offering* to *Almighty God, we pray* inclusive and the concluding doxology may be sung.

B. Eucharistic Prayer II

179. The prayer, *Lord, you are holy indeed,* is said by the principal celebrant alone, with hands outstretched.

180. From *Let your Spirit come* to *May all of us who share* inclusive, all the concelebrants together say the prayer in this manner:
   a. They say *Let your Spirit come* with hands outstretched toward the offerings.
   b. They say *Before he was given up to death* and *When supper was ended* with hands joined.
   c. While saying the words of the Lord, each extends his right hand toward the bread and toward the chalice, if this seems appropriate; they look at the eucharistic bread and the chalice as they are shown and afterward bow low.
   d. They say *In memory of his death* and *May all of us who share* with hands outstretched.

181. The intercessions for the living, *Lord, remember your Church,* and for the dead, *Remember our brothers and sisters,* may be assigned to one of the concelebrants; he alone says the intercessions, with hands outstretched.

182. In this eucharistic prayer the parts from *Before he was given up to death* to *In memory of his death* inclusive and the concluding doxology may be sung.

C. Eucharistic Prayer III

183. The prayer, *Father, you are holy indeed,* is said by the principal celebrant alone, with hands outstretched.

184. From *And so, Father, we bring you these gifts* to *Look with favor* inclusive, all the concelebrants together say the prayer in this manner:
   a. They say *And so, Father, we bring you these gifts* with hands outstretched toward the offerings.
   b. They say *On the night he was betrayed* and *When supper was ended* with hands joined.
   c. While saying the words of the Lord, each extends his right hand toward the bread and toward the chalice, if this seems appropriate; they look at the eucharistic bread and chalice as these are shown and afterward bow low.

d. They say *Father, calling to mind* and *Look with favor* with hands outstretched.

185. The intercessions, *May he make us an everlasting gift* and *Lord, may this sacrifice*, may be assigned to one of the concelebrants; he alone says these prayers, with hands outstretched.

186. In this eucharistic prayer the parts from *On the night he was betrayed* to *Father calling to mind* inclusive and the concluding doxology may be sung.

D. Eucharistic Prayer IV

187. The prayer, *Father, we acknowledge*, is said by the principal celebrant alone, with hands outstretched.

188. From *Father, may this Holy Spirit* to *Lord, look upon this sacrifice* inclusive, all the concelebrants together say the prayer in this manner:
   a. They say *Father, may this Holy Spirit* with hands outstretched toward the offerings.
   b. They say *He always loved those* and *In the same way* with hands joined.
   c. While saying the words of the Lord, each extends his right hand toward the bread and toward the chalice, if this seems appropriate; they look at the eucharistic bread and chalice as these are shown and afterward bow low.
   d. They say *Father, we now celebrate* and *Lord, look upon this sacrifice* with hands outstretched.

189. The intercessions, *Lord, remember those*, may be assigned to one of the concelebrants; he alone says them, with hands outstretched.

190. In this eucharistic prayer the parts form *He always loved those* to *Father, we now celebrate* inclusive and the concluding doxology may be sung.

191. The concluding doxology of the eucharistic prayer may be sung or said either by the principal celebrant alone or together with all the concelebrants.

COMMUNION RITE

192. Next, with hands joined, the celebrant introduces the Lord's Prayer; with hands outstretched, he then says this prayer itself with the other concelebrants and the congregation.

193. The embolism, *Deliver us*, is said by the principal celebrant alone, with hands outstretched. All the concelebrants together with the congregation say the final acclamation, *For the kingdom*.

194. After the deacon (or one of the concelebrants) says: *Let us offer each other the sign of peace*, all exchange the sign of peace. The concelebrants who are nearer the principal celebrant receive the sign of peace from him ahead of the deacon.

195. During the *Agnus Dei*, some of the concelebrants may help the principal celebrant break the eucharistic bread for communion, both for the concelebrants and for the congregation.

196. After the commingling, the principal celebrant alone says softly the prayer, *Lord Jesus Christ, Son of the Living God*, or *Lord Jesus Christ, with faith in your love and mercy*.

197. After this prayer, the principal celebrant genuflects and steps back a little. One by one the concelebrants come to the middle of the altar, genuflect, and reverently take the body of Christ from the altar. Then holding the eucharistic bread in the right hand, with the left hand under it, they return to their places. The concelebrants may, however, remain in their places and take the body of Christ from the paten presented to them by the principal celebrant or by one or more of the concelebrants, or from the paten as it is passed from one to the other.

198. Then the principal celebrant takes the eucharistic bread, holds it slightly raised above the paten, and, facing the congregation, says: *This is the Lamb of God*. With the concelebrants and the congregation he continues: *Lord, I am not worthy*.

199. Then the principal celebrant, facing the altar, says softly: *May the body of Christ bring me to everlasting life* and reverently consumes the body of Christ. The concelebrants do the same. After them the deacon receives the body of Christ from the principal celebrant.

200. The blood of the Lord may be taken by drinking from the chalice directly, through a tube, with a spoon, or even by intinction.

201. If communion is received directly from the chalice, either of two procedures may be followed.
   a. The principal celebrant takes the chalice and says quietly: *May the blood of Christ bring me to everlasting life*. He drinks a little and hands the chalice to the deacon or a concelebrant. Then he gives communion to the faithful or returns to the chair. The concelebrants approach the altar one by one or, if two chalices are used, two by two. They drink the blood of Christ and return to their seats. The deacon or a concelebrant wipes the chalice with a purificator after each concelebrant communicates.
   b. The principal celebrant stands at the middle of the altar and drinks the blood of Christ in the usual manner.

   But the concelebrants may receive the blood of the Lord while remaining in their places. They drink from the chalice presented by the deacon or by one of their number, or else passed from one to the other. Either the one who drinks from the chalice or the one who presents it always wipes it off. After communicating, each one returns to his seat.

202. If communion is received through a tube, this is the procedure. The principal celebrant takes the tube and says softly: *May the blood of Christ bring me to everlasting life.* He drinks a little and immediately cleans the tube by sipping some water from a container at hand on the altar, then places the tube on the paten. The deacon or one of the concelebrants puts the chalice at a convenient place in the middle of the altar or at the right side on another corporal. A container of water for purifying the tubes is placed near the chalice, with a paten to hold them afterward.

The concelebrants come forward one by one, take a tube, and drink a little from the chalice. They then purify the tube, by sipping a little water, and place it on the paten.

203. If communion is received by using a spoon, the same procedure is followed as for communion with a tube. But care is to be taken that after each communion the spoon is placed in a container of water. After communion has been completed, the acolyte carries this container to a side table to wash and dry the spoons.

204. The deacon receives communion last. He then drinks what remains in the chalice and takes it to the side table. There he or the acolyte washes and dries the chalice and arranges it in the usual way.

205. The concelebrants may also receive from the chalice at the altar immediately after receiving the body of the Lord.

In this case the principal celebrant receives under both kinds as he would when celebrating Mass alone, but for the communion from the chalice he follows the rite that in each instance has been decided on for the concelebrants.

After the principal celebrant's communion, the chalice is placed on another corporal at the right side of the altar. The concelebrants come forward one by one, genuflect, and receive the body of the Lord; then they go to the side of the altar and drink the blood of the Lord, following the rite decided upon, as has just been said.

The communion of the deacon and the purification of the chalice take place as already described.

206. If the concelebrants receive communion by intinction, the principal celebrant receives the body and blood of the Lord in the usual way, making sure that enough remains in the chalice for their communion. Then the deacon or one of the concelebrants arranges the paten with the eucharistic bread and the chalice conveniently in the center of the altar or at the right side on another corporal. The concelebrants approach the altar one by one, genuflect, and take a particle, dip part of it into the chalice, and, holding a paten under their chin, communicate. Afterward they return to their places as at the beginning of Mass.

The deacon receives communion also by intinction and to the concelebrant's words: *The body and blood of Christ,* makes the response: *Amen.* At the altar the deacon drinks all that remains in the chalice, takes it to the side table and there he or the acolyte purifies and dries it, then arranges it in the usual way.

CONCLUDING RITE

207. The principal celebrant does everything else until the end of Mass in the usual way; the other concelebrants remain at their seats.

208. Before leaving, the concelebrants make the proper reverence to the altar; as a rule, the principal celebrant kisses the altar.

III. MASS WITHOUT A CONGREGATION
INTRODUCTION

209. This section gives the norms for Mass celebrated by a priest with only one server to assist him and to make the responses.

210. In general this form of Mass follows the rite of Mass with a congregation. The server takes the people's part to the extent possible.

211. Mass should not be celebrated without a server or the participation of at least one of the faithful, except for some legitimate and reasonable cause. In this case the greetings and the blessing at the end of Mass are omitted.

212. The chalice is prepared before Mass, either on a side table near the altar or on the altar itself; the missal is placed on the left side of the altar.

INTRODUCTORY RITES

213. After he reverences the altar, the priest crosses himself, saying: *In the name of the Father*, etc. He turns to the server and gives one of the forms of greeting. For the penitential rite the priest stands at the foot of the altar.

214. The priest then goes up to the altar and kisses it, goes to the missal at the left side of the altar, and remains there until the end of the general intercessions.

215. He reads the entrance antiphon and says the *Kyrie* and the *Gloria*, in keeping with the rubrics.

216. Then, with hands joined, the priest says: *Let us pray*. After a suitable pause, he says the opening prayer, with hands outstretched. At the end the server responds: *Amen*.

LITURGY OF THE WORD

217. After the opening prayer, the server or the priest himself reads the first reading and psalm, the second reading, when it is to be said, and the *Alleluia* verse or other chant.

218. The priest remains in the same place, bows and says: *Almighty God, cleanse my heart*. He then reads the gospel and at the conclusion kisses the

book, saying: *May the words of the gospel wipe away our sins*. The server says the acclamation.

219. The priest then says the profession of faith with the server, if the rubrics call for it.

220. The general intercessions may be said even in this form of Mass; the priest gives the intentions and the server makes the response.

LITURGY OF THE EUCHARIST

221. The antiphon for the preparation of the gifts is omitted. The minister places the corporal, purificator, and chalice on the altar, unless they have already been put there at the beginning of Mass.

222. Preparation of the bread and wine, including the pouring of the water, are carried out as at a Mass with a congregation, with the formularies given in the Order of Mass. After placing the bread and wine on the altar, the priest washes his hands at the side of the altar as the server pours the water.

223. The priest says the prayer over the gifts and the eucharistic prayer, following the rite described for Mass with a congregation.

224. The Lord's Prayer and the embolism, *Deliver us*, are said as at Mass with a congregation.

225. After the acclamation concluding the embolism, the priest says the prayer, *Lord Jesus Christ, you said*. He then adds: *The peace of the Lord be with you always*, and the server answers: *And also with you*. The priest may give the sign of peace to the server.

226. Then, while he says the *Agnus Dei* with the server, the priest breaks the eucharistic bread over the paten. After the *Agnus Dei*, he places a particle in the chalice, saying softly: *May this mingling*.

227. After the commingling, the priest says softly the prayer, *Lord Jesus Christ, Son of the Living God*, or *Lord Jesus Christ, with faith in your love and mercy*. Then he genuflects and takes the eucharistic bread. If the server is to receive communion, the priest turns to him and, holding the eucharistic bread a little above the paten, says: *This is the Lamb of God*, adding once with the server: *Lord, I am not worthy*. Facing the altar, the priest then receives the body of Christ. If the server is not receiving communion, the priest, after making a genuflection, takes the host and, facing the altar, says once quietly: *Lord, I am not worthy*, and eats the body of Christ. The blood of Christ is received in the way described in the Order of Mass with a congregation.

228. Before giving communion to the server, the priest says the communion antiphon.

229. The chalice is washed at the side of the altar and then may be carried by the server to a side table or left on the altar, as at the beginning.

230. After the purification of the chalice, the priest may observe a period of silence. Then he says the prayer after communion.

CONCLUDING RITES

231. The concluding rites are carried out as at Mass with a congregation, but the dismissal formulary is omitted.

IV. SOME GENERAL RULES FOR ALL FORMS OF MASS
VENERATION OF THE ALTAR
AND THE BOOK OF THE GOSPELS

232. According to traditional liturgical practice, the altar and the Book of the Gospels are kissed as a sign of veneration. But if this sign of reverence is not in harmony with the traditions or the culture of the region, the conference of bishops may substitute some other sign, after informing the Apostolic See.

GENUFLECTIONS AND BOWS

233. Three genuflections are made during Mass: after the showing of the eucharistic bread, after the showing of the chalice, and before communion.

If there is a tabernacle with the blessed sacrament in the sanctuary, a genuflection is made before and after Mass and whenever anyone passes in front of the blessed sacrament.

234. There are two kinds of bow, a bow of the head and a bow of the body:
   a. A bow of the head is made when the three divine Persons are named together and at the name of Jesus, Mary and the saint in whose honor Mass is celebrated.
   b. A bow of the body, or profound bow, is made: toward the altar if there is no tabernacle with the blessed sacrament; during the prayers, *Almighty God, cleanse* and *Lord God, we ask you to receive;* within the profession of faith at the words, *by the power of the Holy Spirit;* in Eucharistic Prayer I (Roman Canon) at the words, *Almighty God, we pray.* The same kind of bow is made by the deacon when he asks the blessing before the gospel. In addition, the priest bends over slightly as he says the words of the Lord at the consecration.

INCENSATION

235. The use of incense is optional in any form of Mass:
   a. during the entrance procession;
   b. at the beginning of Mass, to incense the altar;
   c. at the procession and proclamation of the gospel;
   d. at the preparation of the gifts, to incense them, as well as the altar, priest, and people;
   e. at the showing of the eucharistic bread and chalice after the consecration.

236. The priest puts the incense in the censer and blesses it with the sign of the cross, saying nothing.

This is the way to incense the altar:

a. If the altar is freestanding, the priest incenses it as he walks around it.

b. If the altar is not freestanding, he incenses it while walking first to the right side, then to the left.

If there is a cross on or beside the altar, he incenses it before he incenses the altar. If the cross is behind the altar, the priest incenses it when he passes in front of it.

PURIFICATIONS

237. Whenever a particle of the eucharistic bread adheres to his fingers, especially after the breaking of the bread or the communion of the people, the priest cleanses his fingers over the paten or, if necessary, washes them. He also gathers any particles that may fall outside the paten.

238. The vessels are purified by the priest or else by the deacon or acolyte after the communion or after Mass, if possible at a side table. Wine and water or water alone are used for the purification of the chalice, then drunk by the one who purifies it. The paten is usually to be wiped with the purificator.

239. If the eucharistic bread or any particle of it should fall, it is to be picked up reverently. If any of the precious blood spills, the area should be washed and the water poured into the sacrarium.

COMMUNION UNDER BOTH KINDS

240. Holy communion has a more complete form as a sign when it is received under both kinds. For in this manner of reception a fuller light shines on the sign of the eucharistic banquet. Moreover there is a clearer expression of that will by which the new and everlasting covenant is ratified in the blood of the Lord and of the relationship of the eucharistic banquet to the eschatological banquet in the Father's kingdom.[68]

241. For the faithful who take part in the rite or are present at it, pastors should take care to call to mind as clearly as possible Catholic teaching according to the Council of Trent on the manner of communion. Above all they should instruct the people that according to Catholic faith Christ, whole and entire, as well as the true sacrament are received even under one kind only; that, therefore, as far as the effects are concerned, those who receive in this manner are not deprived of any grace necessary for salvation.[69]

Pastors are also to teach that the Church has power in its stewardship of the sacraments, provided their substance remains intact. The Church may make those rules and changes that, in view of the different conditions, times, and places, it decides to be in the interest of reverence for the sacraments or the well-being of the recipients.[70] At the same time the faithful should be guided toward a desire to take part more intensely in a sacred rite in which the sign of the eucharistic meal stands out more explicitly.

242. At the discretion of the Ordinary and after the prerequisite catechesis, communion from the chalice is permitted in the case of:[71]

1. newly baptized adults at the Mass following their baptism; adults at the Mass at which they receive confirmation; baptized persons who are being received into the full communion of the Church;
2. the bride and bridegroom at their wedding Mass;
3. deacons at the Mass of their ordination;
4. an abbess at the Mass in which she is blessed; those consecrated to a life of virginity at the Mass of their consecration; professed religious, their relatives, friends, and the other members of their community at the Mass of first or perpetual vows or renewal of vows;
5. those who receive institution for a certain ministry at the Mass of their institution; lay missionary helpers at the Mass in which they publicly receive their mission; others at the Mass in which they receive an ecclesiastical mission;
6. the sick person and all present at the time viaticum is to be administered when Mass is celebrated in the sick person's home;
7. the deacon and ministers who exercise their office at Mass;
8. when there is a concelebration, in the case of:
   a. all who exercise a liturgical function at this concelebration and also all seminarians present;
   b. in their churches or oratories, all members of institutes professing the evangelical counsels and other societies whose members dedicate themselves to God by religious vows or by an offering or promise; also all those who reside in the houses of members of such institutes and societies;
9. priests who are present at major celebrations and are not able to celebrate or concelebrate;
10. all who make a retreat at a Mass in which they actively participate and which is specially celebrated for the group; also all who take part in the meeting of any pastoral body at a Mass they celebrate as a group;
11. those listed in nos. 2 and 4, at Masses celebrating their jubilees;
12. godparents, relatives, wife or husband, and lay catechists of newly baptized adults at the Mass of their initiation;
13. relatives, friends, and special benefactors who take part in the Mass of a newly ordained priest;
14. members of communities at the conventual or community Mass, in accord with the provisions of this Instruction no. 76.

Further, the conferences of bishops have the power to decide to what extent and under what considerations and conditions Ordinaries may allow communion under both kinds in other instances that are of special significance in the spiritual life of any community or group of the faithful.

Within such limits, Ordinaries may designate the particular instances, but on condition that they grant permission not indiscriminately but for clearly defined celebrations and that they point out matters for caution. They are also to exclude occasions when there will be a large number of communicants. The groups receiving this permission must also be specific, well-ordered, and homogeneous.

243. Preparations for giving communion under both kinds:
    a. If communion is received from the chalice with a tube, silver tubes are needed for the celebrant and each communicant. There should also be a container of water for purifying the tubes and a paten on which to put them afterward.
    b. If communion is given with a spoon, only one spoon is necessary.
    c. If communion is given by intinction, care is to be taken that the eucharistic bread is not too thin or too small, but a little thicker than usual so that after being partly dipped into the precious blood it can still easily be given to the communicant.

1. RITE OF COMMUNION UNDER BOTH KINDS DIRECTLY FROM THE CHALICE

244. If there is a deacon or another assisting priest or an acolyte:
    a. The celebrant receives the Lord's body and blood as usual, making sure enough remains in the chalice for the other communicants. He wipes the outside of the chalice with a purificator.
    b. The priest gives the chalice with purificator to the minister and himself takes the paten or ciborium with the hosts; then both station themselves conveniently for the communion of the people.
    c. The communicants approach, make the proper reverence, and stand in front of the priest. Showing the host he says: *The body of Christ.* The communicant answers: *Amen* and receives the body of Christ from the priest.
    d. The communicant then moves to the minister of the chalice and stands before him. The minister says: *The blood of Christ*, the communicant answers: *Amen*, and the minister holds out the chalice with purificator. For the sake of convenience, communicants may raise the chalice to their mouth themselves. Holding the purificator under the mouth with one hand, they drink a little from the chalice, taking care not to spill it, and then return to their place. The minister wipes the outside of the chalice with the purificator.
    e. The minister places the chalice on the altar after all who are receiving under both kinds have drunk from it. If there are others who are not receiving communion under both kinds, the priest gives these communion, then returns to the altar. The priest or minister drinks whatever remains in the chalice and carries out the usual purifications.

245. If there is no deacon, other priest, or acolyte:

a. The priest receives the Lord's body and blood as usual, making sure enough remains in the chalice for the other communicants. He wipes the outside of the chalice with the purificator.

b. The priest then stations himself conveniently for communion and distributes the body of Christ in the usual way to all who are receiving under both kinds. The communicants approach, make the proper reverence, and stand in front of the priest. After receiving the body of Christ, they step back a little.

c. After all have received, the celebrant places the ciborium on the altar and takes the chalice with the purificator. All those receiving from the chalice come forward again and stand in front of the priest. He says: *The blood of Christ*, the communicant answers: *Amen*, and the priest presents the chalice with purificator. The communicants hold the purificator under their mouth with one hand, taking care that none of the precious blood is spilled, drink a little from the chalice, and then return to their place. The priest wipes the outside of the chalice with the purificator.

d. After the communion from the chalice, the priest places it on the altar and if there are others receiving under one kind only, he gives them communion in the usual way, then returns to the altar. He drinks whatever remains in the chalice and carries out the usual purifications.

2. *RITE OF COMMUNION UNDER BOTH KINDS BY INTINCTION*

246. If there is a deacon, another priest assisting, or an acolyte present:

a. The priest hands this minister the chalice with purificator and he himself takes the paten or ciborium with the hosts. The priest and the minister of the chalice station themselves conveniently for distributing communion.

b. The communicants approach, make the proper reverence, stand in front of the priest, and hold the communion plate below their chin. The celebrant dips a particle into the chalice and, showing it, says: *The body and blood of Christ*. The communicants respond: *Amen*, receive communion from the priest, and return to their place.

c. The communion of those who do not receive under both kinds and the rest of the rite take place as already described.

247. If there is no deacon, assisting priest, or acolyte present:

a. After drinking the blood of the Lord, the priest takes the ciborium, or paten with the hosts, between the index and middle fingers of one hand and holds the chalice between the thumb and index finger of the same hand. Then he stations himself conveniently for communion.

b. The communicants approach, make the proper reverence, stand in front of the priest, and hold a plate beneath their chin. The priest takes a particle, dips it into the chalice, and, showing it, says: *The body and blood of Christ*. The communicants respond: *Amen*, receive communion from the priest, and return to their place.

c. It is also permitted to place a small table covered with a cloth and corporal at a suitable place. The priest places the chalice or ciborium on the table in order to make the distribution of communion easier.

d. The communion of those who do not receive under both kinds, the consumption of the blood remaining in the chalice, and the purifications take place as already described.

3. RITE OF COMMUNION UNDER BOTH KINDS USING A TUBE

248. In this case the priest celebrant also uses a tube when receiving the blood of the Lord.

249. If there is a deacon, another assisting priest, or an acolyte present:
   a. For the communion of the body of the Lord, everything is done as described in nos. 224 b and c.
   b. The communicant goes to the minister of the chalice and stands in front of him. The minister says: *The blood of Christ* and the communicant responds: *Amen*. The communicant receives the tube from the minister, places it in the chalice, and drinks a little. The communicant then removes the tube, careful not to spill any drops, and places it in a container of water held by the minister. The communicant sips a little water to purify the tube, then puts it into another container presented by the minister.

250. If there is no deacon, other assisting priest, or acolyte present, the priest celebrant offers the chalice to each communicant in the way described already for communion from the chalice (no. 245). The minister standing next to him holds the container of water for purifying the tube.

4. RITE OF COMMUNION UNDER BOTH KINDS USING A SPOON

251. If a deacon, another assisting priest, or an acolyte is present, he holds the chalice and, saying: *The blood of Christ*, ministers the blood of the Lord with a spoon to the individual communicants, who hold the plate beneath their chin. He is to take care that the spoon does not touch the lips or tongue of the communicants.

252. If there is no deacon, other assisting priest, or acolyte present, the priest celebrant himself gives them the Lord's blood, after all receiving communion under both kinds have received the Lord's body.

CHAPTER V
ARRANGEMENT AND FURNISHING
OF CHURCHES
FOR THE EUCHARISTIC CELEBRATION

I. GENERAL PRINCIPLES

253. For the celebration of the eucharist, the people of God normally assemble in a church or, if there is none, in some other fitting place worthy of so great a mystery. Churches and other places of worship should therefore be suited to celebrating the liturgy and to ensuring the active participation of the faithful. Further, the places and requisites for worship should be truly worthy and beautiful, signs and symbols of heavenly realities.[72]

254. At all times, therefore, the Church seeks out the service of the arts and welcomes the artistic expressions of all peoples and regions.[73] The Church is intent on keeping the works of art and the treasures handed down from the past[74] and, when necessary, on adapting them to new needs. It strives as well to promote new works of art that appeal to the contemporary mentality.[75]

In commissioning artists and choosing works of art that are to become part of a church, the highest artistic standard is therefore to be set, in order that art may aid faith and devotion and be true to the reality it is to symbolize and the purpose it is to serve.[76]

255. All churches are to be solemnly dedicated or at least blessed. But cathedral and parish churches are always to be dedicated. The faithful should give due honor to the cathedral of their diocese and to their own church as symbols of the spiritual Church that their Christian vocation commits them to build up and extend.

256. All who are involved in the construction, restoration, and remodeling of churches are to consult the diocesan commission on liturgy and art. The local Ordinary is to use the counsel and help of this commission whenever it comes to laying down norms on this matter, approving plans for new buildings, and making decisions on the more important issues.[77]

II. ARRANGEMENT OF A CHURCH FOR THE LITURGICAL ASSEMBLY

257. The people of God assembled at Mass possess an organic and hierarchical structure, expressed by the various ministries and actions for each part

of the celebration. The general plan of the sacred edifice should be such that in some way it conveys the image of the gathered assembly. It should also allow the participants to take the place most appropriate to them and assist all to carry out their individual functions properly.

The congregation and the choir should have a place that facilitates their active participation.[78]

The priest and his ministers have their place in the sanctuary, that is, in the part of the church that brings out their distinctive role, namely, to preside over the prayers, to proclaim the word of God, or to minister at the altar.

Even though these elements must express a hierarchical arrangement and the diversity of offices, they should at the same time form a complete and organic unity, clearly expressive of the unity of the entire holy people. The character and beauty of the place and all its appointments should foster devotion and show the holiness of the mysteries celebrated there.

III. SANCTUARY

258. The sanctuary should be clearly marked off from the body of the church either by being somewhat elevated or by its distinctive design and appointments. It should be large enough to accommodate all the rites.[79]

IV. ALTAR

259. At the altar the sacrifice of the cross is made present under sacramental signs. It is also the table of the Lord and the people of God are called together to share in it. The altar is, as well, the center of the thanksgiving that the eucharist accomplishes.[80]

260. In a place of worship, the celebration of the eucharist must be on an altar, either fixed or movable. Outside a place of worship, especially if the celebration is only for a single occasion, a suitable table may be used, but always with a cloth and corporal.

261. A fixed altar is one attached to the floor so that it cannot be moved; a movable altar is one that can be transferred from place to place.

262. In every church there should ordinarily be a fixed, dedicated altar, which should be freestanding to allow the ministers to walk around it easily and Mass to be celebrated facing the people. It should be so placed as to be a focal point on which the attention of the whole congregation centers naturally.[81]

263. According to the Church's traditional practice and the altar's symbolism, the table of a fixed altar should be of stone and indeed of natural stone. But at the discretion of the conference of bishops some other solid, becoming, and well-crafted material may be used.

The pedestal or base of the table may be of any sort of material, as long as it is becoming and solid.

264. A movable altar may be constructed of any becoming, solid material suited to liturgical use, according to the traditions and customs of different regions.

265. Altars both fixed and movable are dedicated according to the rite described in the liturgical books; but movable altars may simply be blessed.

266. The practice of placing under the altar to be dedicated relics of saints, even of nonmartyrs, is to be maintained. Care must be taken to have solid evidence of the authenticity of such relics.

267. Other altars should be fewer in number. In new churches they should be placed in chapels separated in some way from the body of the church.[82]

V. ALTAR FURNISHINGS

268. At least one cloth should be placed on the altar out of reverence for the celebration of the memorial of the Lord and the banquet that gives us his body and blood. The shape, size, and decoration of the altar cloth should be in keeping with the design of the altar.

269. Candles are to be used at every liturgical service as a sign of reverence and festiveness. The candlesticks are to be placed either on or around the altar in a way suited to the design of the altar and the sanctuary. Everything is to be well balanced and must not interfere with the faithful's clear view of what goes on at the altar or is placed on it.

270. There is also to be a cross, clearly visible to the congregation, either on the altar or near it.

VI. CHAIR FOR THE PRIEST CELEBRANT AND THE MINISTERS, THAT IS, THE PLACE WHERE THE PRIEST PRESIDES

271. The priest celebrant's chair ought to stand as a symbol of his office of presiding over the assembly and of directing prayer. Thus the best place for the chair is at the back of the sanctuary and turned toward the congregation, unless the structure or other circumstances are an obstacle (for example, if too great a distance would interfere with communication between the priest and people). Anything resembling a throne is to be avoided. The seats for the ministers should be so placed in the sanctuary that they can readily carry out their appointed functions.[83]

VII. LECTERN (AMBO) OR PLACE FROM WHICH THE WORD OF GOD IS PROCLAIMED

272. The dignity of the word of God requires the church to have a place that is suitable for proclamation of the word and is a natural focal point for the people during the liturgy of the word.[84]

As a rule the lectern or ambo should be stationary, not simply a movable stand. In keeping with the structure of each church, it must be so placed that the ministers may be easily seen and heard by the faithful.

The readings, responsorial psalm, and the Easter Proclamation (*Exsultet*) are proclaimed from the lectern; it may be used also for the homily and general intercessions (prayer of the faithful).

It is better for the commentator, cantor, or choir director not to use the lectern.

VIII. PLACES FOR THE FAITHFUL

273. The places for the faithful should be arranged with care so that the people are able to take their rightful part in the celebration visually and mentally. As a rule, there should be benches or chairs for their use. But the custom of reserving seats for private persons must be abolished.[85] Chairs or benches should be set up in such a way that the people can easily take the positions required during various celebrations and have unimpeded access to receive communion.

The congregation must be enabled not only to see the priest and the other ministers but also, with the aid of modern sound equipment, to hear them without difficulty.

IX. CHOIR, ORGAN, AND OTHER MUSICAL INSTRUMENTS

274. In relation to the design of each church, the *schola cantorum* should be so placed that its character as a part of the assembly of the faithful that has a special function stands out clearly. The location should also assist the choir's liturgical ministry and readily allow each member complete, that is, sacramental participation in the Mass.[86]

275. The organ and other lawfully approved musical instruments are to be placed suitably in such a way that they can sustain the singing of the choir and congregation and be heard with ease when they are played alone.

X. RESERVATION OF THE EUCHARIST

276. Every encouragement should be given to the practice of eucharistic reservation in a chapel suited to the faithful's private adoration and prayer.[87] If this is impossible because of the structure of the church, the sacrament should be reserved at an altar or elsewhere, in keeping with local custom, and in a part of the church that is worthy and properly adorned.[88]

277. The eucharist is to be reserved in a single, solid, immovable tabernacle that is opaque and is locked in such a way as to provide every possible security against the danger of desecration. Thus as a rule there should be only one tabernacle in each church.[89]

XI. IMAGES FOR VENERATION BY THE FAITHFUL

278. In keeping with the Church's very ancient tradition, it is lawful to set up in places of worship images of Christ, Mary, and the saints for veneration by the faithful. But there is need both to limit their number and to situate them in such a way that they do not distract the people's attention from the celebration.[90] There is to be only one image of any one saint. In general, the devotion of the entire community is to be the criterion regarding images in the adornment and arrangement of a church.

XII. GENERAL PLAN OF THE CHURCH

279. The style in which a church is decorated should be a means to achieve noble simplicity, not ostentation. The choice of materials for church appointments must be marked by concern for genuineness and by the intent to foster instruction of the faithful and the dignity of the place of worship.

280. Proper planning of a church and its surroundings that meets contemporary needs requires attention not only to the elements belonging directly to liturgical services but also to those facilities for the comfort of the people that are usual in places of public gatherings.

CHAPTER VI
REQUISITES FOR CELEBRATING MASS

I. BREAD AND WINE

281. Following the example of Christ, the Church has always used bread and wine with water to celebrate the Lord's Supper.

282. The bread must be made only from wheat and must have been baked recently; according to the long-standing tradition of the Latin Church, it must be unleavened.

283. The nature of the sign demands that the material for the eucharistic celebration truly have the appearance of food. Accordingly, even though unleavened and baked in the traditional shape, the eucharistic bread should be made in such a way that in a Mass with a congregation the priest is able actually to break the host into parts and distribute them to at least some of the faithful. (When, however, the number of communicants is large or other pastoral needs require it, small hosts are in no way ruled out.) The action of the breaking of the bread, the simple term for the eucharist in apostolic times, will more clearly bring out the force and meaning of the sign of the unity of all in the one bread and of their charity, since the one bread is being distributed among the members of one family.

284. The wine for the eucharist must be from the fruit of the vine (see Lk 22:18), natural, and pure, that is not mixed with any foreign substance.

285. Care must be taken to ensure that the elements are kept in good condition: that the wine does not turn to vinegar or the bread spoil or become too hard to be broken easily.

286. If the priest notices after the consecration or as he receives communion that water instead of wine was poured into the chalice, he pours the water into another container, then pours wine with water into the chalice and consecrates it. He says only the part of the institution narrative related to the consecration of the chalice, without being obliged to consecrate the bread again.

II. SACRED FURNISHINGS IN GENERAL

287. As in the case of architecture, the Church welcomes the artistic style of every region for all sacred furnishings and accepts adaptations in keeping with the genius and traditions of each people, provided they fit the purpose for which the sacred furnishings are intended.[91]

In this matter as well the concern is to be for the noble simplicity that is the perfect companion of genuine art.

288. In the choice of materials for sacred furnishings, others besides the traditional are acceptable that by contemporary standards are considered to be of high quality, are durable, and well suited to sacred uses. The conference of bishops is to make the decisions for each region.

III. SACRED VESSELS

289. Among the requisites for the celebration of Mass, the sacred vessels hold a place of honor, especially the chalice and paten, which are used in presenting, consecrating, and receiving the bread and wine.

290. Vessels should be made from materials that are solid and that in the particular region are regarded as noble. The conference of bishops will be the judge in this matter. But preference is to be given to materials that do not break easily or become unusable.

291. Chalices and other vessels that serve as receptacles for the blood of the Lord are to have a cup of nonabsorbent material. The base may be of any other solid and worthy material.

292. Vessels that serve as receptacles for the eucharistic bread, such as a paten, ciborium, pyx, monstrance, etc., may be made of other materials that are prized in the region, for example, ebony or other hard woods, as long as they are suited to sacred use.

293. For the consecration of hosts one rather large paten may properly be used; on it is placed the bread for the priest as well as for the ministers and the faithful.

294. Vessels made from metal should ordinarily be gilded on the inside if the metal is one that rusts; gilding is not necessary if the metal is more precious than gold and does not rust.

295. The artist may fashion the sacred vessels in a shape that is in keeping with the culture of each region, provided each type of vessel is suited to the intended liturgical use.

296. For the blessing or consecration of vessels the rites prescribed in the liturgical books are to be followed.

IV. VESTMENTS

297. In the Church, the Body of Christ, not all members have the same function. This diversity of ministries is shown outwardly in worship by the

diversity of vestments. These should therefore symbolize the function proper to each ministry. But at the same time the vestments should also contribute to the beauty of the rite.

298. The vestment common to ministers of every rank is the alb, tied at the waist with a cincture, unless it is made to fit without a cincture. An amice should be put on first if the alb does not completely cover the street clothing at the neck. A surplice may not be substituted for the alb when the chasuble or dalmatic is to be worn or when a stole is used instead of the chasuble or dalmatic.

299. Unless otherwise indicated, the chasuble, worn over the alb and stole, is the vestment proper to the priest celebrant at Mass and other rites immediately connected with Mass.

300. The dalmatic, worn over the alb and stole, is the vestment proper to the deacon.

301. Ministers below the order of deacon may wear the alb or other vestment that is lawfully approved in each region.

302. The priest wears the stole around his neck and hanging down in front. The deacon wears it over his left shoulder and drawn across the chest to the right side, where it is fastened.

303. The cope is worn by the priest in processions and other services, in keeping with the rubrics proper to each rite.

304. Regarding the design of vestments, the conferences of bishops may determine and propose to the Apostolic See adaptations that correspond to the needs and usages of their regions.[92]

305. In addition to the traditional materials, natural fabrics proper to the region may be used for making vestments; artificial fabrics that are in keeping with the dignity of the liturgy and the person wearing them may also be used. The conference of bishops will be the judge in this matter.[93]

306. The beauty of a vestment should derive from its material and design rather than from lavish ornamentation. Representations on vestments should consist only of symbols, images, or pictures portraying the sacred. Anything out of keeping with the sacred is to be avoided.

307. Variety in the color of the vestments is meant to give effective, outward expression to the specific character of the mysteries of the faith being celebrated and, in the course of the year, to a sense of progress in the Christian life.

308. Traditional usage should be retained for the vestment colors.
   a. White is used in the offices and Masses of the Easter and Christmas seasons; on feasts and memorials of the Lord, other than of his passion; on feasts and memorials of Mary, the angels, saints who

were not martyrs, All Saints (1 November), John the Baptist (24 June), John the Evangelist (27 December), the Chair of St. Peter (22 February), and the Conversion of St. Paul (25 January).

b. Red is used on Passion Sunday (Palm Sunday) and Good Friday, Pentecost, celebrations of the Lord's passion, birthday feasts of the apostles and evangelists, and celebrations of martyrs.

c. Green is used in the offices and Masses of Ordinary Time.

d. Violet is used in Lent and Advent. It may also be worn in offices and Masses for the dead.

e. Black may be used in Masses for the dead.

f. Rose may be used on *Gaudete* Sunday (Third Sunday of Advent) and *Laetare* Sunday (Fourth Sunday of Lent).

The conference of bishops may choose and propose to the Apostolic See adaptations suited to the needs and culture of peoples.

309. On solemn occasions more precious vestments may be used, even if not of the color of the day.

310. Ritual Masses are celebrated in their proper color, in white, or in a festive color; Masses for various needs and occasions are celebrated in the color proper to the day or the season or in violet if they bear a penitential character, for example, ritual Masses nos. 23, 28, and 40; votive Masses are celebrated in the color suited to the Mass itself or in the color proper to the day or season.

V. OTHER REQUISITES FOR CHURCH USE

311. Besides vessels and vestments for which some special material is prescribed, any other furnishings that either have a liturgical use or are in any other way introduced into a church should be worthy and suited to their particular purpose.

312. Even in minor matters, every effort should be made to respect the canons of art and to combine cleanliness and a noble simplicity.

CHAPTER VII
CHOICE OF THE MASS AND ITS PARTS

313. The pastoral effectiveness of a celebration will be heightened if the texts of readings, prayers, and songs correspond as closely as possible to the needs, religious dispositions, and aptitude of the participants. This will be achieved by an intelligent use of the broad options described in this chapter.

In planning the celebration, then, the priest should consider the general spiritual good of the assembly rather than his personal outlook. He should be mindful that the choice of texts is to be made in consultation with the ministers and others who have a function in the celebration, including the faithful in regard to the parts that more directly belong to them.

Since a variety of options is provided for the different parts of the Mass, it is necessary for the deacon, readers, psalmists, cantors, commentator, and choir to be completely sure beforehand of those texts for which they are responsible so that nothing is improvised. A harmonious planning and execution will help dispose the people spiritually to take part in the eucharist.

I. CHOICE OF MASS

314. On solemnities the priest is bound to follow the calendar of the church where he is celebrating.

315. On Sundays, on weekdays of Advent, the Christmas season, Lent, and the Easter season, on feasts, and on obligatory memorials:
   a. if Mass is celebrated with a congregation, the priest should follow the calendar of the church where he is celebrating;
   b. if Mass is celebrated without a congregation, the priest may choose either the calendar of the church or his own calendar.

316. On optional memorials:
   a. On the weekdays of Advent from 17 December to 24 December, during the octave of Christmas, and on the weekdays of Lent, apart from Ash Wednesday and in Holy Week, the priest celebrates the Mass of the day; but he may take the opening prayer from a memorial listed in the General Roman Calendar for that day, except on Ash Wednesday and during Holy Week.

b. On the weekdays of Advent before 17 December, the weekdays of the Christmas season from 2 January on, and the weekdays of the Easter season, the priest may choose the weekday Mass, the Mass of the saint or of one of the saints whose memorial is observed, or the Mass of a saint inscribed in the martyrology for that day.

c. On the weekdays in Ordinary Time, the priest may choose the weekday Mass, the Mass of an optional memorial, the Mass of a saint inscribed in the martyrology for that day, a Mass for various needs and occasions, or a votive Mass.

If he celebrates with a congregation, the priest should first consider the spiritual good of the faithful and avoid imposing his own personal preferences. In particular, he should not omit the readings assigned for each day in the weekday lectionary too frequently or without sufficient reason, since the Church desires that a richer portion of God's word be provided for the people.[94]

For similar reasons he should use Masses for the dead sparingly. Every Mass is offered for both the living and the dead and there is a remembrance of the dead in each eucharistic prayer.

Where the faithful are attached to the optional memorials of Mary or the saints, at least one Mass of the memorial should be celebrated to satisfy their devotion.

When an option is given between a memorial in the General Roman Calendar and one in a diocesan or religious calendar, the preference should be given, all things being equal and depending on tradition, to the memorial in the particular calendar.

II. CHOICE OF INDIVIDUAL TEXTS

317. In the choice of texts for the several parts of the Mass, the following rules are to be observed. They apply to Masses of the season and of the saints.

READINGS

318. Sundays and holydays have three readings, that is, from the Old Testament, from the writings of an apostle, and from a Gospel. Thus God's own teaching brings the Christian people to a knowledge of the continuity of the work of salvation.

Accordingly, it is expected that there will be three readings, but for pastoral reasons and by decree of the conference of bishops the use of only two readings is allowed in some places. In such a case, the choice between the first two readings should be based on the norms in the Lectionary and on the intention to lead the people to a deeper knowledge of Scripture; there should never be any thought of choosing a text because it is shorter or easier.

319. In the weekday lectionary, readings are provided for each day of every week throughout the year; therefore, unless a solemnity or feast occurs, these readings are for the most part to be used on the days to which they are assigned.

The continuous reading during the week, however, is sometimes interrupted by the occurrence of a feast or particular celebration. In this case the priest, taking into consideration the entire week's plan of readings, is allowed either to combine omitted parts with other readings or to give preference to certain readings.

In Masses with special groups, the priest may choose texts more suited to the particular celebration, provided they are taken from the texts of an approved lectionary.

320. The Lectionary has a special selection of texts from Scripture for Masses that incorporate certain sacraments or sacramentals or that are celebrated by reason of special circumstances.

These selections of readings have been assigned so that by hearing a more pertinent passage from God's word the faithful may be led to a better understanding of the mystery they are taking part in and may be led to a more ardent love for God's word.

Therefore the texts for proclamation in the liturgical assembly are to be chosen on the basis of their pastoral relevance and the options allowed in this matter.

PRAYERS

321. The many prefaces enriching the Roman Missal are intended to develop in different ways the theme of thanksgiving in the eucharistic prayer and bring out more clearly the different facets of the mystery of salvation.

322. The choice of the eucharistic prayer may be guided by the following norms.

a. Eucharistic Prayer I, the Roman Canon, which may be used on any day, is particularly apt on days when there is a special text for the prayer, *In union with the whole Church* or in Masses that have a special form of the prayer, *Father, accept this offering;* also on the feasts of the apostles and saints mentioned in it and on Sundays, unless for pastoral considerations another eucharistic prayer is preferred.

b. Eucharistic Prayer II has features that make it particularly suitable for weekdays and special circumstances.

Although it has its own preface, it may also be used with other prefaces, especially those that summarize the mystery of salvation, such as the Sunday prefaces or the common prefaces.

When Mass is celebrated for a dead person, the special formulary may be inserted in the place indicated, namely, before the intercession, *Remember our brothers and sisters.*

c. Eucharistic Prayer III may be said with any preface. Its use is particularly suited to Sundays and holydays.

The special formulary for a dead person may be used with this prayer in the place indicated, namely, at the prayer, *In mercy and love unite all your children.*

d. Eucharistic Prayer IV has a fixed preface and provides a fuller summary of the history of salvation. It may be used when a Mass has no preface of its own.

Because of the structure of this prayer no special formulary for the dead may be inserted.

e. A eucharistic prayer that has its own preface may be used with that preface, even when the Mass calls for the preface of the season.

323. In any Mass the prayers belonging to that Mass are used, unless otherwise noted.

In Masses on a memorial, however, the opening prayer or collect may be from the Mass itself or from the common; the prayer over the gifts and prayer after communion, unless they are proper, may be taken either from the common or from the weekdays of the current season.

On the weekdays in Ordinary Time, the prayers may be taken from the preceding Sunday, from another Sunday in Ordinary Time, or from the prayers for various needs and occasions listed in the Missal. It is always permissible even to use the opening prayer from these Masses.

This provides a rich collection of texts that create an opportunity continually to rephrase the themes of prayer for the liturgical assembly and also to adapt the prayer to the needs of the people, the Church, and the world. During the more important seasons of the year, however, the proper seasonal prayers appointed for each day in the Missal already make this adaptation.

SONG

324. The norms laid down in their proper places are to be observed for the choice of chants between the readings and the songs for the processions at the entrance, presentation of the gifts, and communion.

SPECIAL PERMISSIONS

325. In addition to the permissions just given to choose more suitable texts, the conferences of bishops have the right in some circumstances to make further adaptations of readings, but on condition that the texts are taken from an approved lectionary.

CHAPTER VIII
MASSES AND PRAYERS FOR VARIOUS NEEDS AND OCCASIONS AND MASSES FOR THE DEAD

I. MASSES AND PRAYERS FOR VARIOUS NEEDS AND OCCASIONS

326. For well-disposed Christians the liturgy of the sacraments and sacramentals causes almost every event in human life to be made holy by divine grace that flows from the paschal mystery.[95] The eucharist, in turn, is the sacrament of sacraments. Accordingly, the Missal provides formularies for Masses and prayers that may be used in the various circumstances of Christian life, for the needs of the whole world, and for the needs of the Church, both local and universal.

327. In view of the broad options for choosing the readings and prayers, the Masses for various needs and occasions should be used sparingly, that is, when the occasion requires.

328. In all the Masses for various needs and occasions, unless otherwise indicated, the weekday readings and the chants between them may be used, if they are suited to the celebration.

329. The Masses for various needs and occasions are of three types:
   a. the ritual Masses, which are related to the celebration of certain sacraments or sacramentals;
   b. the Masses for various needs and occasions, which are used either as circumstances arise or at fixed times;
   c. the votive Masses of the mysteries of the Lord or in honor of Mary or a particular saint or of all the saints, which are options provided in favor of the faithful's devotion.

330. Ritual Masses are prohibited on the Sundays of Advent, Lent, and the Easter season, on solemnities, on days within the octave of Easter, on All Souls, on Ash Wednesday, and during Holy Week. In addition, the norms in the ritual books or in the Masses themselves also apply.

331. From the selection of Masses for various needs and occasions, the competent authority may choose Masses for those special days of prayer that the conferences of bishops may decree during the course of the year.

332. In cases of serious need or pastoral advantage, at the direction of the local Ordinary or with his permission, an appropriate Mass may be celebrated on any day except solemnities, the Sundays of Advent, Lent, and the Easter season, days within the octave of Easter, on All Souls, Ash Wednesday, and during Holy Week.

333. On obligatory memorials, on the weekdays of Advent until 16 December, of the Christmas season after 2 January, and of the Easter season after the octave of Easter, Masses for various needs and occasions are per se forbidden. But if some real need or pastoral advantage requires, at the discretion of the rector of the church or the priest celebrant, the Masses corresponding to such need or advantage may be used in a celebration with a congregation.

334. On weekdays in Ordinary Time when there is an optional memorial or the office is of that weekday, any Mass or prayer for various needs and occasions is permitted, but ritual Masses are excluded.

II. MASSES FOR THE DEAD

335. The Church offers Christ's paschal sacrifice for the dead so that on the basis of the communion existing between all Christ's members, the petition for spiritual help on behalf of some members may bring others comforting hope.

336. The funeral Mass has first place among the Masses for the dead and may be celebrated on any day except solemnities that are days of obligation, Holy Thursday, the Easter triduum, and the Sundays of Advent, Lent, and the Easter season.

337. On the occasions of news of a death, final burial, or the first anniversary, Mass for the dead may be celebrated even on days within the Christmas octave, on obligatory memorials, and on weekdays, except Ash Wednesday and during Holy Week.

Other Masses for the dead, that is, daily Masses, may be celebrated on weekdays in Ordinary Time when there is an optional memorial or the office is of the weekday, provided such Masses are actually offered for the dead.

338. At the funeral Mass there should as a rule be a short homily, but never a eulogy of any kind. The homily is also recommended at other Masses for the dead celebrated with a congregation.

339. All the faithful, and especially the family, should be urged to share in the eucharistic sacrifice offered for the deceased person by receiving communion.

340. If the funeral Mass is directly joined to the burial rite, once the prayer after communion has been said and omitting the rite of dismissal, the rite of final commendation or of farewell takes place, but only when the body is present.

341. In the planning and choosing of the variable parts of the Mass for the dead, especially the funeral Mass (for example, prayers, readings, general intercessions) pastoral considerations bearing upon the deceased, the family, and those attending should rightly be foremost.

Pastors should, moreover, take into special account those who are present at a liturgical celebration or hear the Gospel only because of the funeral. These may be non-Catholics or Catholics who never or rarely share in the eucharist or who have apparently lost the faith. Priests are, after all, ministers of Christ's Gospel for all people.

NOTES

This translation of the GIRM is not based on the Latin text accompanying the 1969 *Ordo Missae*, but rather that in the 1975 *editio typica altera* of the *Missale Romanum*. Three versions of the GIRM preceded that accompanying the *editio typica altera*: 1) The GIRM issued with the new *Ordo Missae* promulgated 6 April 1969; 2) The GIRM as emended in the *editio typica* of the *Missale Romanum*, promulgated 26 March 1970; 3) The GIRM as emended by the variations published by the Sacred Congregation for Divine Worship 23 December 1972, following the suppression of the diaconate and minor orders by the *motu proprio Ministeria quaedam*, 15 August 1972.

[ABBREVIATIONS USED IN THE NOTES:]

CD   Vatican Council II, *Christus Dominus* (Decree on the Pastoral Office of Bishops in the Church), 28 October 1965.

CIC   *Codex Iuris Canonici* (Code of Canon Law).

DV   Vatican Council II, *Dei verbum* (Dogmatic Constitution on Divine Revelation), 18 November 1965.

EuchMyst   Sacred Congregation of Rites, instruction *Eucharisticum mysterium* (Instruction on Eucharistic Worship), 25 May 1967.

GILH   Sacred Congregation of Divine Worship, *Institutio Generalis de Liturgia Horarum* (General Instruction on the Liturgy of the Hours), 2 February 1971.

InterOec   Sacred Congregation of Rites, instruction *Inter Oecumenici*, 26 September 1964.

LG   Vatican Council II, *Lumen gentium* (Dogmatic Constitution on the Church), 21 November 1964.

MusSacr   Sacred Congregation of Rites, instruction *Musicam sacram*, 5 March 1967.

PL   Migne, J.-P. (ed.), *Patrologia latina* (Paris 1844-64).

PO   Vatican Council II, *Presbyterorum ordinis* (Decree on the Ministry and Life of Presbyters), 7 December 1965.

RR   Roman Ritual.

SacraVeron Mohlberg, L.C. (ed.), *Sacramentarium Veronese* (Rome 1955).

SC   Vatican Council II, *Sacrosanctum Concilium* (Constitution on the Sacred Liturgy), 4 December 1963.

SCDS   Sacred Congregation for the Discipline of the Sacraments.

SCDW   Sacred Congregation for Divine Worship.

SCR   Sacred Congregation of Rites.

UR   Vatican Council II, *Unitatis redintegratio* (Decree on Ecumenism), 21 November 1964.

[INTRODUCTION]

[1]See Council of Trent, sess. 22, 17 Sept. 1562: Denz-Schön 1738-59.

[2]SC art. 47; see LG nos. 3, 28; PO nos. 2, 4, 5.

[3]Mohlberg SacrVeron no. 93.

[4]See Eucharistic Prayer III.

[5]See Eucharistic Prayer IV.

[6]See SC art. 7, 47; PO nos. 5, 18.

[7]See Pius XII, Encycl. *Humani generis:* AAS 42(1950) 570-571. Paul VI, Encycl. *Mysterium fidei* nos. 33-35; Solemn Profession of Faith, 30 June 1968, nos. 24-26. SCR, Instr. EuchMyst, 25 May 1967, nos. 3, 9.

[8]See Council of Trent, sess. 13, 11 Oct. 1551: Denz-Schön 1635-61.

[9]See PO no. 2.

[10]See SC art. 11.

[11]SC art. 50.

[12]Council of Trent, sess. 22, *Doctr. de SS. Missae Sacrificio* cap. 8: Denz-Schön 1749.

[13]Ibid. can. 9: Denz-Schön 1759.

[14]Ibid. cap. 8: Denz-Schön 1749.

[15]See SC art. 33.

[16]See SC art. 36.

[17]See SC art. 52.

[18]See SC art. 35, 3.

[19]SC art. 55.

[20]Council of Trent, sess. 22, *Doctr. de SS. Missae Sacrificio* cap. 6: Denz-Schön 1747.

[21]See SC art. 55.

[CHAPTER I]

[1]See SC art. 41; LG no. 11; PO nos. 2, 5, 6; CD no. 30; UR no. 15. SCR, Instr. EuchMyst, 25 May 1967, nos. 3e, 6.

[2]See SC art. 10.

[3]See SC art. 102.

[4]See PO no. 5; SC art. 10.

[5]See SC art. 14, 19, 26, 28, 30.

[6]See SC art. 47.

[7]See SC art. 14.

[8]See SC art. 41.

[9]See PO no. 13.

[10]See SC art. 59.

[11]For Masses with special groups see SCDW, Instr. *Actio pastoralis* 15 May 1969; for Masses with children, SCDW, *Directory for Masses with Children*, 1 Nov. 1973; for the manner of joining the liturgy of the hours with the Mass, GILH nos. 93-98.

[12]See SC art. 37-40.

[CHAPTER II]

[13] See PO no. 5.

[14]See Council of Trent, sess. 22, cap. 1: Denz-Schön 1740. Paul VI, Solemn Profession of Faith, 30 June 1968, no. 24.

[15]See SC art. 7. Paul VI, Encycl. *Mysterium fidei*, 3 Sept. 1965. SCR, Instr. EuchMyst, 25 May 1967, no. 9.

[16]See SC art. 56. SCR, Instr. EuchMyst no. 10.

[17]See SC art. 48, 51; DV no. 21; PO no. 4.

[18]See SC art. 7, 33, 52.

[19]See SC art. 33.

[20]See SCDW, Circular letter on the eucharistic prayers, 27 April 1973, no. 14.

[21]See SCR, Instr. MusSacr. 5 March 1967, no. 14.

[22]See SC art. 26, 27.

[23]See SC art. 30.

[24]See SCR, Instr. MusSacr no. 16a.

[25]Augustine, *Sermo* 336, 1: PL 38, 1472.

[26]See SCR, MusSacr nos. 7, 16. MR, *Ordo cantus Missae*, ed. typica, 1972, Introduction.

[27]See SC art. 54. SCR, Instr. InterOec, 26 Sept. 1964, no. 59; Instr. MusSacr no. 47.

[28]See SC art. 30.

[29]See SC art. 39.

[30]See SC art. 30. SCR, Instr. MusSacr no. 17.

[31]See SC art. 33.

[32]See SC art. 7.

[33]See SC art. 51.

[34]See SCR, InterOec no. 50.

[35]See SC art. 52.

[36]See SCR, Instr, InterOec no. 54.

[37]See ibid. no. 56.

[38]See SC art. 53.

[39]See SCR, Instr. InterOec no. 56.

[40]See SC art. 47. SCR, Instr. EuchMyst no. 3a, b.

[41]See SCR, Instr. InterOec no. 91.

[42]See SC art. 48; PO no. 5. SCR, Instr. EuchMyst no. 12.

[43]See SCR, Instr. EuchMyst nos. 12, 33a.

[44]See SCR, Instr. EuchMyst, 25 May 1967, on communion twice in one day, nos. 31, 32: AAS 59 (1967), pp. 558, 559. See also CIC, can. 917.

[CHAPTER III]

[45]See SC art. 14, 26.

[46]See SC art. 28.

[47]See LG nos. 26, 28; SC art. 42.

[48]See SC art. 26.

[49]See PO no. 2; LG no. 28.

[50]See SC art. 48. SCR, Instr. EuchMyst no. 12.

[51]See SCR, Instr. MusSacr no. 19.

[52]See ibid. no. 21.

[53]See SC art. 24.

[54]See SCDS, Instr. *Immensae caritatis*, 29 Jan. 1973, no. 1.

[55]See SCDW, Instr. *Liturgicae instaurationes*, 5 Sept. 1970, no. 7.

[CHAPTER IV]

[56]See SC art. 41.

[57]See SC art. 42. SCR, Instr. EuchMyst 25 May 1967, no. 26. LG no. 28; PO no. 5.

[58]See SCR, Instr. EuchMyst no. 47. SCDW, Decl. on concelebration, 7 Aug. 1972.

[59]See SCR, Instr. EuchMyst no. 26; Instr. MusSacr, 5 March 1967, nos. 16, 27.

[60]See SCDW, Decr., 9 Oct. 1972.

[61]See Paul VI, Motu Proprio *Ministeria quaedam*, 15 Aug. 1972, no. VI.

[62]See SC art. 57; CIC, can. 902.

[63]See SCR, Instr. EuchMyst no. 47.

[64]See *Rite of Concelebration*, Introduction no. 3.

[65]See ibid. no. 8.

[66]See SCR, Decr. *Ecclesiae semper*, 7 *March 1965; Instr. EuchMyst no. 47.*

[67]See *Rite of Concelebration*, Introduction no. 9. SCDW, Decl. on concelebration 7 Aug. 1972.

[68]See SCR, Instr. EuchMyst no. 32.

[69]See Council of Trent, sess. 21, Decr. *De Communione eucharistica* cap. 1-3: Denz-Schön 1725-29.

[70]See ibid. cap. 2: Denz-Schön 1728.

[71]See SCDW, Instr. *Sacramentali Communione*, 29 June 1970.

[CHAPTER V]

[72]See SC art. 122-124; PO no. 5. SCR, Instr. InterOec, 26 Sept. 1964, no. 90; Instr. EuchMyst, 25 May 1967, no. 24.

[73]See SC art. 123.

[74]See SCR, Instr. EuchMyst no. 24.

[75]See SC art. 123, 129. SCR, Instr. InterOec no. 13c.

[76]See SC art. 123.

[77]See SC art. 126.

[78]See SCR, InterOec nos. 97-98.

[79]See ibid. no. 91.

[80]See SCR, Instr. EuchMyst no. 24.

[81]See SCR, Instr. InterOec no. 91.

[82]See ibid. no. 93.

[83]See ibid. no. 92.

[84]See ibid. no. 96.

[85]See SC art. 32. SCR, Instr. InterOec no. 98.

[86]See SCR, Instr. MusSacr no. 23.

[87]See SCR, Instr. EuchMyst no. 53. RR, *Holy Communion and Worship of the Eucharist outside Mass*, *ed. typica*, 1973, Introduction no. 9.

[88]See SCR, Instr. EuchMyst no. 54; Instr. InterOec no. 95.

[89]See SCR, Instr. EuchMyst no. 52; Instr. InterOec no. 95. SC Sacraments, Instr. *Nullo umquam tempore*, 28 May 1938, no. 4: AAS 30 (1938) 199–200. RR, *Holy Communion and Worship of the Eucharist outside Mass*, Introduction nos. 10–11; CIC, can. 938.

[90]See SC art. 125.

[CHAPTER VI]

[91]See SC art. 128. SCR, Instr. EuchMyst, 25 May 1967, no. 24.

[92]See SC art. 128.

[93]See ibid.

[CHAPTER VII]

[94]See SC art. 51.

[CHAPTER VIII]

[95]See SC art. 61.

APPENDIX 1

APPENDIX TO THE *GENERAL INSTRUCTION* FOR THE DIOCESES OF THE UNITED STATES OF AMERICA

The following notes, related to the individual sections of the *General Instruction of the Roman Missal*, include adaptations made by the National Conference of Catholic Bishops for the dioceses of the United States, as well as supplementary references.

For further documentation concerning the Eucharistic celebration, see Congregation of Rites, *Instruction on Eucharistic Worship* (May 25, 1967), especially "Some General Principles of Particular Importance in the Catechesis of the People on the Mystery of the Eucharist" (nos. 5-15) and "The Celebration of the Memorial of the Lord" (nos. 16-48); and Sacred Congregation for the Sacraments and Divine Worship, *On Certain Norms concerning Worship of the Eucharistic Mystery* (April 17, 1980).

The number at the beginning of each section below refers to the respective section of the *General Instruction*. Unless otherwise indicated, decisions of the National Conference of Catholic Bishops were taken at the plenary session of November, 1969.

11. INTRODUCTIONS AND INVITATIONS

With regard to the adaptation of words of introduction, see the circular letter of the Congregation for Divine Worship, April 27, 1973. No. 14 reads:

Among the possibilities for further accommodating any individual celebration, it is important to consider the admonitions, the homily and the general intercessions. First of all are the admonitions. These enable the people to be drawn into a fuller understanding of the sacred action, or any of its parts, and lead them into a true spirit of participation. The *General Instruction of the Roman Missal* entrusts the more important admonitions to the priest for preparation and use. He may introduce the Mass to the people before the celebration begins, during the liturgy of the word prior to the actual readings, and in the Eucharistic prayer before the preface; he may also conclude the entire sacred action before the dismissal. The *Order of Mass* provides others as well, which are important to certain portions of the rite, such as during the penitential rite, or before the Lord's Prayer. By their very nature these brief admonitions do not require that everyone use them in the form in which they appear in the *Missal*. Provision can be made in certain cases that they be adapted to some degree to the varying circumstances of the community. In all cases it is well to remember the nature of an admonition, and not make them into a sermon or homily; care should be taken to keep them brief and not too wordy, for otherwise they become tedious.

19. SINGING

See the statement of the Bishops' Committee on the Liturgy, *The Place of Music in Eucharistic Celebrations* (Washington, 1968); revised ed., *Music in Catholic Worship* (Washington, 1972).

The settings for liturgical texts to be sung by the priest and ministers that are given in the *Sacramentary* are chant adaptations prepared by the International Commission on English in the Liturgy, rather than new melodies. Other settings for the ministerial chants are those approved by the National Conference of Catholic Bishops (November, 1965).

No official approbation is needed for new melodies for the Lord's Prayer at Mass or for the chants, acclamations and other song of the congregation.

In accord with no. 55 of the instruction of the Congregation of Rites on music in the liturgy (March 5, 1967), the Conference of Bishops has determined that vernacular texts set to music composed in earlier periods may be used in liturgical services even though they may not conform in all details with the legitimately approved versions of liturgical texts (November, 1967). This decision authorizes the use of choral and other music in English when the older text is not precisely the same as the official version.

21. ACTIONS AND POSTURES

At its meeting in November, 1969, the National Conference of Catholic Bishops voted that in general, the directives of the *Roman Missal* concerning the posture of the congregation at Mass should be left unchanged, but that no. 21 of the *General Instruction* should be adapted so that the people kneel beginning after the singing or recitation of the Sanctus until after the Amen of the Eucharistic prayer, that is, before the Lord's Prayer.

26. ENTRANCE SONG

As a further alternative to the singing of the entrance antiphon and psalm of the *Roman Gradual (Missal)* or of the *Simple Gradual*, the Conference of Bishops has approved the use of other collections of psalms and antiphons in English, as supplements to the Simple Gradual, including psalms arranged in responsorial form, metrical and similar versions of psalms, provided they are used in accordance with the principles of the Simple Gradual and are selected in harmony with the liturgical season, feast or occasion (decree confirmed by the Consilium for the Implementation of the Constitution on the Liturgy, December 17, 1968).

With regard to texts of other sacred songs from the psalter that may be used as the entrance song, the following criterion was adopted by the Conference of Bishops in November, 1969:

> The entrance rite should create an atmosphere of celebration. It serves the function of putting the assembly in the proper frame of mind for listening to the word of God. It helps people to become conscious of themselves as a worshiping community. The choice of texts for the entrance song should not conflict with these purposes.
>
> In general, during the most important seasons of the Church year, Easter time, Lent, Christmas and Advent, it is preferable that most songs used at the entrance be seasonal in nature.

There are thus four options for the entrance song:
1. the entrance antiphon and psalm of the *Roman Gradual;*
2. the entrance antiphon and psalm of the *Simple Gradual;*
3. song from other collections of psalms and antiphons;
4. other sacred song chosen in accord with the above criterion.

The same options exist for the sacred song at the offertory and Communion, but not for the chants between the readings (below).

Only if none of the above alternatives is employed and there is no entrance song, is the antiphon in the Missal recited.

36. CHANTS BETWEEN THE READINGS

As a further alternative to (1) the singing of the psalm with its response in the *Lectionary*, (2) the gradual in the *Roman Gradual*, or (3) the responsorial or alleluia psalm in the *Simple Gradual*, the Conference of Bishops has approved the use of other collections of psalms and antiphons in English, as supplements to the *Simple Gradual*, including psalms arranged in responsorial form, metrical and similar versions of psalms, provided they are used in accordance with the principles of the *Simple Gradual* and are selected in harmony with the liturgical season, feast or occasion (decree confirmed by the Consilium for the Implementation of the Constitution on the Liturgy, December 17, 1968).

The choice of texts that are *not* from the psalter (permitted at the entrance, offertory and Communion) is not extended to the chants between the readings.

For further information concerning the use of the chants between the readings, see the Foreword and the Introduction (VIII) to the *Lectionary for Mass* (New York, Collegeville, Minn., 1970). In particular, see the common texts for sung responsorial psalms (nos. 174-175), which may be used in place of the text corresponding to the reading whenever the psalm is sung.

During Lent the alleluia is not sung with the verse before the Gospel. Instead one of the following (or similar) acclamations may be sung before and after the verse before the Gospel:

Praise and honor to you, Lord Jesus Christ,

King of endless glory!
Praise and honor to you, Lord Jesus Christ!
Glory and praise to you, Lord Jesus Christ!
Glory to you, Word of God, Lord Jesus Christ!

If the psalm after the reading is not sung, it is recited. The alleluia or the verse before the Gospel may be omitted if not sung (see no. 39 of the *General Instruction*). The people stand for the singing of the alleluia before the Gospel (see no. 21 of the *General Instruction*).

45. GENERAL INTERCESSIONS

See the statement of the Bishops' Committee on the Liturgy, *General Prayer or Prayer of the Faithful*, July, 1969.

50. OFFERTORY SONG

The choice of texts for the offertory song is governed by the same rule as the entrance song, with the several options described above (no. 26). If there is no offertory song, the offertory antiphon is omitted.

With regard to texts not from the psalter that may be used as the offertory song, the following criterion was adopted by the National Conference of Bishops in November, 1969:

The offertory song need not speak of bread and wine or of offering. The proper function of the offertory song is rather to accompany and celebrate the communal aspects of the procession. The text, therefore, may be an appropriate song of praise or of rejoicing in keeping with the season. Those texts are not acceptable that speak of the offering completely apart from the action of Christ.

In general, during the most important seasons of the Church year, Easter time, Lent, Christmas and Advent, it is preferable that most songs used during the offertory be seasonal in character. During the remainder of the Church year, however, topical songs may be used during the offertory procession provided that these texts do not conflict with the paschal character of every Sunday *(Constitution on the Liturgy*, arts. 102, 106).

With regard to the offertory song, the statement of the Bishops' Committee on the Liturgy of 1968 *(The Place of Music in Eucharistic Celebrations)* gives additional comments:

The procession can be accompanied by song. Song is not always necessary or desirable. Organ or instrumental music is also fitting at this time. The song need not speak of bread or wine or offering. The proper function of this song is to accompany and celebrate the communal aspects of the procession. The text, therefore, can be any appropriate song of praise or of rejoicing in keeping with the season. (See approved criterion above.) The song need not accompany the entire preparation rite. (The song, if any, continues at least until the priest has placed the bread and wine on the altar, while saying the accompanying prayers quietly; see no. 50 of the *General Instruction*, nos. 19-21 of the *Order of Mass.*)

If there is no singing or organ or instrumental music, this may be a period of silence (see no. 23 of the *General Instruction*). In fact, it is good to give the assembly a period of quiet (that is, while the gifts are prepared and placed on the altar, until the introduction to the prayer over the gifts: "Pray, brethren. . .") before demanding, at the preface, their full attention to the Eucharistic prayer.

56b. SIGN OF PEACE

The Conference of Bishops has left the development of specific modes of exchanging the sign of peace to local usage. Neither a specific form nor specific words are determined (November, 1969).

56i. COMMUNION SONG

The choice of texts for the Communion song is governed by the same rule as the entrance song, with the several options described above (no. 26).

With regard to the texts not from the psalter that may be used as the Communion song, the following criterion was adopted by the National Conference of Catholic Bishops in November, 1969:

The Communion song should foster a sense of unity. It should be simple and not demand great effort. It gives expression to the joy of unity in the body of Christ and the fulfillment of the mystery being celebrated. Most benediction hymns, by reason of their concentration on adoration rather than on Communion, are not acceptable, as indicated in the instruction on music in the liturgy, no. 36.

In general, during the most important seasons of the Church year, Easter time, Lent, Christmas and Advent, it is preferable that most songs used at the Communion be seasonal in nature. During the remainder of the Church year, however, topical songs may be used during the Communion procession provided these texts do not conflict with the paschal character of every Sunday *(Constitution on the Liturgy*, arts. 102, 106).

Only if none of the above alternatives is employed and there is no Communion song, is the antiphon in the *Missal* recited. Until the publication of the complete new *Missal*, the antiphon from the present *Missal* is said in such cases (Congregation for Divine Worship, instruction, October 20, 1969, no. 13).

59. CELEBRATION BY THE BISHOP

See Congregation of Rites, instruction on the simplification of pontifical rites and insignia, June 21, 1968.

For occasions when the bishop is present at a celebration of the Eucharist but, for a just reason, does not elect to be the principal celebrant, he may assign another to celebrate the liturgy of the Eucharist while he presides over the introductory rites, the liturgy of the word and the concluding rite of the Mass. For directives on the manner in which this is done, see *Newsletter* of the Bishops' Committee on the Liturgy, May-June, 1981.

66. WOMEN AS READERS

The Conference of Bishops has given permission for women to serve as readers in accord with no. 66 of the *General Instruction* (November, 1969).

In February, 1971, the Bishops' Committee on the Liturgy prepared a commentary on the liturgical ministry of women:

    a. With the exception of service at the altar itself, women may be admitted to the exercise of other liturgical ministries. In particular the designation of women to serve in such ministries as reader, cantor, leader of singing, commentator, director of liturgical participation, etc., is left to the judgment of the pastor or the priest who presides over the celebration, in the light of the culture and mentality of the congregation.

    b. Worthiness of life and character and other qualifications are required in women who exercise liturgical ministries in the same way as for men who exercise the same ministries.

    c. Women who read one or other biblical reading during the liturgy of the word (other than the Gospel, which is reserved to a deacon or priest) should do so from the lectern or ambo where the other readings are proclaimed: the reservation of a single place for all the biblical readings is more significant than the person of the reader, whether ordained or lay, whether woman or man (cf. *General Instruction*, no 272).

    d. Other ministries performed by women, such as leading the singing or otherwise directing the congregation, should be done either within or outside the sanctuary area, depending on circumstances or convenience.

127. OFFICE OF DEACON

The various ministries of the deacon at Mass may be distributed among several deacons, present and wearing their vestments. (See Congregation of Rites, instruction, June 21, 1968, nos. 4, 5.) Other deacons who are present but not called upon to function in the celebration normally should not vest or occupy a specific place in the liturgy, unless they are participating as the *order of deacons*, e.g., at the liturgy of ordination of another deacon. (See Bishops' Committee on the Liturgy, *Newsletter*, October, 1981.)

153. CONCELEBRATED MASS

See the statement of the Bishops' Committee on the Liturgy, "Concelebration," *Newsletter*, June, 1966.

240. DISTRIBUTION OF COMMUNION

On June 17, 1977, the Congregation of Sacraments and Divine Worship approved the request of the National Conference of Catholic Bishops to permit the optional practice of Communion in the hand. The Bishops' Committee on the Liturgy, in its catechesis about this optional practice, drew attention to these considerations:

    a. Proper catechesis must be provided to assure the proper and reverent reception of Communion without any suggestion of wavering on the part of the Church in its faith in the Eucharistic presence.

    b. The practice must remain the option of the communicant. The priest or minister of Communion does not make the decision as to the manner of reception of Communion. It is the communicant's personal choice.

    c. When Communion is distributed under both kinds by intinction, the host is not placed in the hands of the communicants, nor may the communicants receive the host and dip it into the chalice. Intinction should not be introduced as a means of circumventing the practice of Communion in the hand.

    d. Children have the option to receive Communion in the hand or on the tongue. No limitations because of age have been established. Careful preparation for first reception of the Eucharist will provide the necessary instruction. (See also the Roman Ritual, *Holy Communion and Worship of the Eucharist outside Mass*, no. 21.)

242. COMMUNION UNDER BOTH KINDS

See the statement of the Bishops' Committee on the Liturgy, "Communion under Both Kinds," *Newsletter*, July 1966.

In accord with the instruction of the Congregation for Divine Worship on Communion under both kinds (June 29, 1970), the National Conference of Catholic Bishops in November, 1970, added the following cases:

15. other members of the faithful present on the special occasions enumerated in no. 242 of the *General Instruction;*

16. at funeral Masses and at Masses for a special family observance;

17. at Masses on days of special religious or civil significance for the people of the United States;

18. at Masses on Holy Thursday and at the Mass of the Easter Vigil, the norms of the instruction of June 29, 1970, being observed;

19. at weekday Masses.

At its meeting in November, 1978, the National Conference of Catholic Bishops further extended the occasions on which Holy Communion under both kinds might be given when it approved the motion that Holy Communion may be given under both kinds to the faithful at Masses on Sundays and holy days of obligation if, in the judgment of the ordinary, Communion may be given in an orderly and reverent manner.

263. MATERIALS FOR FIXED ALTARS

Materials other than natural stone may be used for fixed altars provided these are worthy, solid and properly constructed, subject to the further judgment of the local ordinary in doubtful cases.

270. ALTAR CROSS

Only a single cross should be carried in a procession in order to give greater dignity and reverence to the cross. It is desirable to place the cross that has been carried in the procession near the altar so that it may serve as the cross of the altar. Otherwise it should be put away during the service. (See Congregation of Rites, instruction, June 21, 1968, no. 20.)

275. MUSICAL INSTRUMENTS

The Conference of Bishops has decreed that musical instruments other than the organ may be used in liturgical services provided they are played in a manner that is suitable to public worship (November, 1967; see *Constitution on the Liturgy*, art. 120). This decision deliberately refrains from singling out specific instruments. Their use depends on circumstances, the nature of the congregation, etc. In particular cases, if there should be doubt as to the suitability of the instruments, it is the responsibility of the diocesan bishop, in consultation with the diocesan liturgical and music commissions, to render a decision.

288. MATERIALS FOR SACRED FURNISHINGS

Materials other than the traditional ones may be used for sacred furnishings provided they are suitable for liturgical use, subject to the further judgment of the local ordinary in doubtful cases.

305. MATERIALS FOR VESTMENTS

Fabrics, both natural and artificial, other than the traditional ones may be used for sacred vesture provided they are suitable for liturgical use, subject to the further judgment of the local ordinary in doubtful cases.

308. COLOR OF VESTMENTS

White, violet or black vestments may be worn at funeral services and at other offices and Masses for the dead (November, 1970).

318. READINGS ON SUNDAYS AND FEASTS

According to the decision of the National Conference of Catholic Bishops, the complete pattern of three readings for Sundays and feast days should be completely implemented.

331. DAYS OF PRAYER

The Conference of Bishops has decreed that there be observed in the dioceses of the United States, at times to be designated by the local ordinary in consultation with the diocesan liturgical commission, days or periods of prayer for the fruits of the earth, prayer for human rights and equality, prayer for world justice and peace, and penitential observance outside Lent (November, 1971). This is in addition to observances customary on certain civic occasions such as Independence Day, Labor Day and Thanksgiving Day, for which either proper text or texts of the *Sacramentary* and *Lectionary for Mass* are provided.

The Bishops' Committee on the Liturgy presented the above decision in these terms: The expression of such days or periods of prayer should be left as general as possible, so that the time, length, occasion, and more specific intentions of prayer should be determined locally rather than nationally. In this way no arbitrary rule is imposed until it becomes evident that a pattern of such supplications is emerging from practice. See also General Norms for the Liturgical Year and the Calendar, nos. 45-47.

340. FUNERAL MASS

Although the rite of final commendation at the catafalque or pall is excluded, it is permitted to celebrate the funeral service, including the commendations, in those cases where it is physically or morally impossible for the body of the deceased person to be present (November, 1970).

For other adaptations in the funeral Mass and service, see the *Rite of Funerals* (1971); *Newsletter* of the Bishops' Committee on the Liturgy, April-May, 1971. The following refer directly to the Eucharistic celebration:

It is appropriate that the paschal candle be carried in the entrance procession.

If the introductory rites have taken place at the church door, the priest venerates the altar and goes to his chair. The penitential rite is omitted, and the priest says or sings the opening prayer.

It is desirable that the first and second readings be read by relatives or friends of the deceased person.

The homily may properly include an expression of praise and gratitude to God for his gifts, particularly the gift of a Christian life, to the deceased person. The homily should relate Christian death to the paschal mystery of the Lord's victorious death and resurrection and to the hope of eternal life.

It is desirable that members of the family or friends of the deceased person participate in the usual offering of the bread and wine for the celebration of the Eucharist, together with other gifts for the needs of the Church and of the poor.

If incense is used, the priest, after incensing the gifts and the altar, may incense the body. The deacon or another minister then incenses the priest and people.

APPENDIX 2
CLARIFICATIONS AND INTERPRETATIONS OF THE *GENERAL INSTRUCTION OF THE ROMAN MISSAL*

The Sacred Congregation for Sacraments and Divine Worship, through its official publication *Notitiae*, has issued a number of clarifications regarding the reformed rites of the Church and their celebration. The interpretations and explanations which affect the *General Instruction of the Roman Missal* and which appeared in *Notitiae* between 1969 and 1981 are included below. The numbers at the beginning of each section refer to the respective sections of the *General Instruction*.

12.   QUERY: An organ accompaniment for the recitation of the eucharistic prayer is a practice that has developed in some places. Is this acceptable?
REPLY: The GIRM no. 12 clearly states: "The nature of the presidential prayers demands that they be spoken in a loud and clear voice and that everyone present listen with attention. While the priest is reciting them there should be no other prayer and the organ or other instruments should not be played." This is a clear rule, leaving no room for doubt, since it is a reminder of wrong practices that have greatly impeded and diminished the people's participation in this central part of the Mass. Further, it is obvious that the organ's so-called background music often puts into the background what should be foremost and dominant. A "background" accompaniment of the priest's homily would be out of the question: but in the eucharistic prayer the word of the presider, *Toū proestoū* in Justin's expression, reaches the peak of its meaning: Not 13 (1977) 94-95, no. 2.

21.   QUERY 1: After communion should the faithful be seated or not?
REPLY: After communion they may either kneel, stand, or sit. Accordingly the GIRM no. 21 gives this rule: "The people sit. . .if this seems useful during the period of silence after communion." Thus it is a matter of option, not obligation. The GIRM no. 121, should, therefore, be interpreted to match no. 21: Not 10 (1974) 407.

QUERY 2: In liturgical assemblies there is a great variety of gestures and postures during a celebration. For example, should the people: a. stand during the prayer over the gifts; b. kneel after the *Sanctus* and during the entire eucharistic prayer; c. sit after communion? **REPLY:** As usual the GIRM gives simple rules to solve these questions (GIRM no. 21): a. The people stand while the presidential prayers are being said, therefore, during the prayer over the gifts. b. They also stand throughout the eucharistic prayer, except the consecration. The practice is for the faithful to remain kneeling from the epiclesis before the consecration until the memorial acclamation after it. c. The people may sit during the silence after communion.

The points determined are in no way to be considered trivial, since their purpose is to ensure uniformity in posture in the assembly celebrating the eucharist as a manifestation of the community's unity in faith and worship. The people often give the impression immediately after the *Sanctus* and even more often after the consecration by their diverse postures that they are unmindful of being participants in the Church's liturgy, which is the supreme action of a community and not a time for individuals to isolate themselves in acts of private devotion: Not 14 (1978) 300-301, no. 1.

QUERY 3: In some places kneelers have been taken out of the churches. Thus, the people can only stand or sit and this detracts from the reverence and adoration due to the eucharist. **REPLY:** The appointments of a place of worship have some relationship to the customs of the particular locale. For example, in the East there are carpets; in the Roman basilicas, only since modern times, there are usually chairs without kneelers, so as to accommodate large crowds. There is nothing to prevent the faithful from kneeling on the floor to show their adoration, no matter how uncomfortable this may be. In cases where kneeling is not possible (see GIRM no. 21), a deep bow and a respectful bearing are signs of the reverence and adoration to be shown at the time of the consecration and communion: Not 14 (1978) 302-303, no. 4.

23.   QUERY 1: Is it appropriate to meditate for a short time in silence after the homily? **REPLY:** Very much so.

QUERY 2: May the organ be played softly during this interval of silence? **REPLY:** Yes, as long as it really is played softly and is *not* a distraction to meditation: Not 9 (1973) 192.

26.   QUERY: In the GIRM no. 26 are the words *actioni sacrae* to be understood of the procession of the priest and ministers or of the entire eucharistic celebration? **REPLY:** The words are to be understood of the procession, because the context is about the entrance song. Nevertheless the norm takes on a general applicability; whatever the singing during Mass, it should fit the character of the season and of the part of the rite actually taking place: Not 6 (1970) 404, no. 42.

29.   QUERY: Does the *Asperges* rite still exist? **REPLY:** Yes. For it is a rite that on Sunday helpfully calls to mind the baptismal washing. But this matter will be settled better in the new missal, in such a way that the *Asperges* will be coordinated with the penitential rite of the Mass: Not 5 (1969) 403, no. 11.

31. **QUERY 1:** What is to be understood by the phrase "a special, more solemn celebration?" **REPLY:** This occasion on which GIRM no. 31 calls for the singing of the *Gloria* is a celebration observed with solemnity or with a large number of people: Not 6 (1970) 263, no. 33.

QUERY 2: When the *Gloria* and *Credo* are not sung but just recited, sometimes the celebrant conducts the recitation in alternation with the congregation. But since a hymn and a profession of faith are at issue and these involve the assembly as a whole, does this practice seem to be keeping with the rubrics? **REPLY:** The rubrics of the Order of Mass, drawn up in a practical fashion, have only this on the *Gloria*: "the hymn is sung or recited" (no. 5) and on the *Credo*: "the profession of faith. . .is made" (no. 15). As is often the case, the GIRM shows progress of a spiritual order (nos. 31 and 43), by bringing out the community character proper to these texts and by stressing the dialogic style for their recitation. a. As to the *Gloria*, the GIRM no. 31, to preserve its character as a hymn, says: "It is sung by the congregation, or by the congregation alternately with the choir, or by the choir alone. If not sung, it is to be recited either by all together or in alternation." By preference, therefore, the *Gloria* should be sung. Otherwise it is recited by all either together or in alternation. The celebrant should join with the assembly's singing or reciting of the *Gloria* together or with one sector of the assembly's dialogic recitation or else he should recite the hymn in alternation with the assembly. b. As to the *Credo*, the GIRM no. 44 says: "Recitation of the profession of faith by the priest together with the people is obligatory on Sundays and solemnities. It may be said also at special, more solemn celebrations. If it is sung, as a rule all are to sing it together or in alternation." Therefore, whether sung or recited the *Credo* belongs to the entire liturgical assembly, which says it together ("all") or sings it as two alternating choirs: Not 14 (1978) 538, no. 14.

42. **QUERY:** Is it advisable to invite the faithful to bless themselves before or after the homily, to address a salutation to them, for example, "Praised be Jesus Christ, etc?" **REPLY:** It all depends on lawful local custom. But generally speaking it is inadvisable to continue such customs because they have their origin in preaching outside Mass. The homily is part of the liturgy; the people have already blessed themselves and received the greeting at the beginning of Mass. It is better, then, not to have a repetition before or after the homily: Not 9 (1973) 178.

44. **QUERY:** Is the *Credo* to be said during the Easter octave? **REPLY:** Not per se; still, it may be said even on these weekdays when there is a "more solemn" celebration: Not 7 (1971) 112, no. 2. See also no. 31, Query 2b above.

49.   QUERY 1: What is the genuine meaning of the offertory rite? The description of the offertory of the Mass, it is pointed out, speaks only of the *preparation* of the gifts and placing them on the altar, of the people's offerings for the Church and for the poor, but nothing about the *offering* of the sacrifice. **REPLY:** History teaches that the offertory rite is an action of preparation for the sacrifice in which priest and ministers accept the gifts offered by the people. These are the elements for the celebration (the bread and wine) and other gifts intended for the Church and the poor. This preparatory meaning has always been regarded as the identifying note of the offertory, even though the formularies did not adequately bring it out and were couched in sacrificial language. The new rite puts this specifying note in a clearer light by means both of the active part taken by the faithful in the presentation of the gifts and the formularies the celebrant says in placing the elements for the eucharistic celebration on the altar: Not 6 (1970) 37, no. 25.

QUERY 2: Does it not seem that the suppression of the prayers that accompanied the offering of the bread and wine has impoverished the offertory rite? **REPLY:** In no way. The former prayers: *Suscipe, Sancte Pater...* and *Offerimus tibi, Domine...* were not accurate expressions of the genuine meaning of the "offertory" rites but merely anticipated the meaning of the true and literal sacrificial offering that is present in the eucharistic prayer after the consecration, when Christ becomes present on the altar as victim. The new formularies for the gifts bring out the giving of glory to God, who is the source of all things and of all the gifts given to humanity. They state explicitly the meaning of the rite being carried out; they associate the value of human work, which embraces all human concerns, with the mystery of Christ. The offertory rite, then, has been restored through that explicit teaching and shines forth with new light: Not 6 (1970) 37-38, no. 26.

51.   QUERY: In Mass with a congregation celebrated more solemnly, different ways of incensation are being used: one plain and simple; the other, the same as the rite for incensation prescribed in the former Roman Missal. Which usage should be followed? **REPLY:** It must never be forgotten that the Missal of Pope Paul VI has, since 1970, supplanted the one called improperly "the Missal of St. Pius V," and completely so, in both texts and rubrics. When the rubrics of the Missal of Paul VI say nothing or say little on particulars in some places, it is not to be inferred that the former rite should be observed. Therefore, the multiple and complex gestures for incensation as prescribed in the former Missal (see *Missale Romanum*, Vatican Polyglot Press, 1962: *Ritus servandus* VIII and *Ordo incensandi* pp. LXXX-LXXXIII) are not to be resumed.

In incensation the celebrant (GIRM nos. 51 and 105) proceeds as follows: a. toward the gifts: he incenses with three swings, as the deacon does toward the Book of the Gospels; b. toward the cross: he incenses with three swings when he comes in front of it; c. toward the altar: he incenses continuously from the side as he passes around the altar, making no distinction between the altar table and the base: Not 14 (1978) 301-302, no. 2.

52. **QUERY:** May the rite of washing the hands be omitted from the celebration of Mass? **REPLY:** In no way. 1. Both the GIRM (nos. 52, 106, 222) and the Order of Mass (with a congregation, no. 24; without a congregation, no. 18) show the *Lavabo* to be one of the prescribed rites in the preparation of the gifts. A rite of major importance is clearly not at issue, but it is not to be dropped since its meaning is: "an expression of the (priest's) desire to be cleansed within" (GIRM no. 52). In the course of the Consilium's work on the Order of Mass, there were a number of debates on the value and the place to be assigned to the *Lavabo*, e.g., on whether it should be a rite in silence or with an accompanying text; there was, however, unanimity that it must be retained. Even though there has been no practical reason for the act of handwashing since the beginning of the Middle Ages, its symbolism is obvious and understood by all (see SC art. 34). The rite is a usage in all liturgies of the West. 2. The Constitution on the Liturgy (SC art. 37-40) envisions ritual adaptations to be suggested by the conferences of bishops and submitted to the Holy See. Such adaptations must be based on serious reasons, for example, the specific culture and viewpoint of a people, contrary and unchangeable usages, the practical impossibility of adapting some new rite that is foreign to the genius of a people, and so on. 3. Apart from the envisioned exemptions from rubrics and differing translations of texts (see Consilium, Instr. 25 Jan. 1969), the Order of Mass is presented as a single unit whose general structure and individual components must be exactly respected. Arbitrary selectiveness on the part of an individual or a community would soon result in the ruin of a patiently and thoughtfully constructed work: Not 6 (1970) 38-39, no. 27.

55d. In certain vernacular versions of the text for consecrating the wine, the words *pro multis* are translated thus: English, *for all*; Spanish, *por todos*; Italian, *per tutti*.

QUERY: a. Is there a sufficient reason for introducing in this variant and if so, what is it? b. Is the pertinent traditional teaching in the *Catechism of the Council of Trent* to be considered superseded? c. Are all other versions of the biblical passage in question to be regarded as less accurate? d. Did something inaccurate and needing correction or emendation in fact slip in when the approval was given for such a version? **REPLY:** The variant involved is fully justified: a. According to exegetes the Aramaic word translated in Latin by *pro multis* has as its meaning "for all": the many for whom Christ died is without limit; it is equivalent to saying "Christ has died for all." The words of St. Augustine are apposite: "See what he gave and you will discover what he bought. The price is Christ's blood. What is it worth but the whole world? What, but all peoples? Those who say either that the price is so small that it has purchased only Africans are ungrateful for the price they cost; those who say that they are so important that it has been given for them alone are proud" (*Enarr. in Ps.* 95, 5). b. The teaching of the *Catechism* is in no way superseded: the distinction that Christ's death is sufficient for all but efficacious for many remains valid. c. In the approval of this vernacular variant in the liturgical text nothing inaccurate has slipped in that requires correction or emendation: Not 6 (1970) 39-40, no. 28.

55g. QUERY: In the intercessions of Eucharistic Prayer III, this parenthesis appears ("Saint N.—the saint of the day or the patron saint"). How should these words be interpreted? Must the saint of the day or the patron saint be mentioned? And even on a Sunday or on more solemn days? May the blessed also be mentioned? **REPLY:** a. The words quoted, as is rightly noted, are in parenthesis; therefore, mention of the saint of the day or the patron saint is to be considered as optional. But it should not be omitted all the time, because mention of the saint adds something concretely relevant to the participants, the place, and the circumstances. b. There may, therefore, always be a mention of the saint of the day or of the patron saint, even if celebration of a Mass in honor of the saint is impeded, and even on Sunday and more solemn days. Special conditions of people and places may sometimes favor omission, for example, if mention of a little-known saint may cause puzzlement. The celebrant should always guard against imposing his own personal devotion on the faithful. c. What has been said about saints is applicable to the blessed, but only in keeping with places and ways established by law (see CIC can. 1277, § 2): Not 14 (1978) 594-595, no. 17.

56e. QUERY 1: May the singing of *Shalom* replace the singing of the *Agnus Dei?* **REPLY:** No. The Ordinary of the Mass in all its parts must be followed as it appears in the Missal. Some slight adaptation is countenanced in the *Directory for Masses with Children* no. 31. What is established for children, however, is not transferable to other assemblies: Not 11 (1975) 205.

QUERY 2: How many times must the *Agnus Dei* be said or sung, according to the indications in the Order of Mass? **REPLY:** The point of the *Agnus Dei* is to accompany the breaking of the consecrated bread until a particle is dropped into the chalice (GIRM no. 56e). In practice two situations are to be considered: a. If there is only one celebrant presiding or if there are only a few concelebrants, the breaking of the bread is done quite quickly. Usually the *Agnus Dei* said or sung three times, as indicated in the Order of Mass no. 131, is enough to accompany the rite. b. In the case when there are many concelebrants or the breaking of the bread takes a long time, then the *Agnus Dei* may be repeated until the completion of the breaking of the bread, following the rubric in the Order of Mass no. 131: "This may be repeated. . ." and the directive of the GIRM no. 56e: "This invocation may be repeated as often as necessary to accompany the breaking of the bread. The final reprise concludes with the words, *grant us peace*": Not 14 (1978) 306, no. 8.

57a. QUERY: What is the formulary a bishop is to use for the final blessing of Mass? **REPLY:** Although nothing is said on this point in the new Order of Mass, at the end of Mass bishops bless the people either with the more solemn formulary that will appear in the new Roman Missal or with the formulary that has been customary until now, namely: *Blessed be the name of the Lord. . .*; *Our help is in the name of the Lord* (they do not cross themselves); *May almighty God bless you. . .*; as he makes the triple sign of the cross: Not 5 (1969) 403, no. 14. See also no. 108 below.

61. See DOL 309 no. 2536, note R.

62. QUERY: Are hand missals still needed? **REPLY:** Since reform of the liturgy the usefulness of hand missals for the faithful is often questioned. All now understand the words spoken at Mass; what is more, as far as the biblical readings are concerned, all ought to be listening attentively to the word of God. Nevertheless hand missals, it seems, remain necessary. People do not always hear well, espeically in large churches, and what they do hear physically they do not always understand right away. They, therefore, often need to go back over the texts heard during a celebration. In addition, the liturgy, and the eucharistic celebration above all, is "the summit toward which the activity of the Church is directed; at the same time it is the fount from which all the Church's power flows" (SC art. 10). All the concerns of the spiritual life must be brought to the liturgy and that happens if participation is truly actual and *aware*. This requires frequent meditation on the liturgical texts both before and after the celebration: Not 8 (1972) 195-196. See also the notes from Bp. R. Coffy, President of the Liturgical Commission of France, and the survey of vernacular missals available: ibid. 196-198.

76. See DOL 223 no. 1796, note R.

79. See no. 269 below.

80c. QUERY: In a great many places the veil is hardly ever used to cover the chalice prepared at a side table before Mass. Have any recent norms been given to suppress use of the veil? **REPLY:** There is no norm, not even a recent one, to change the GIRM no. 80c, which reads: "The chalice should be covered with a veil, which may always be white.": Not 14 (1978) 594, no. 16.

87. QUERY: During the recitation of certain formularies, for example, the *Confiteor, Agnus Dei, Domine, non sum dignus*, the accompanying gestures on the part of both priest and people are not always the same: some strike their breast three times; others, once during such formularies. What is the lawful practice to be followed? **REPLY:** In this case it is helpful to recall: 1. gestures and words usually complement each other; 2. in this matter as in others the liturgical reform has sought authenticity and simplicity, in keeping with SC art. 34: "The rites should be marked by a noble simplicity." Whereas in the Roman Missal promulgated by authority of the Council of Trent meticulous gestures usually accompanied the words, the rubrics of the Roman

Missal as reformed by authority of Vatican Council II are marked by their restraint with regard to gestures. This being said: a. The words, *Through my own fault* in the *Confiteor* are annotated in the reformed Roman Missal with the rubric: "They strike their breast" (*Ordo Missae* no. 3). In the former Missal at the same place the rubric read this way: "He strikes his breast three times." Therefore, it seems that the breast is not to be struck three times by anyone in reciting the words, whether in Latin or another language, even if the tripled formulary is said (*mea culpa, mea culpa, mea maxima culpa*). One striking of the breast is enough. Clearly, also, one gesture is enough in those languages in which the words expressing fault are translated in a simpler form, for example in English, *I have sinned through my own fault*; in French *Oui, j'ai vraiment péché*. b. The special restraint of the reformed Roman Missal is also clear regarding the other texts mentioned, the *Agnus Dei* and *Domine, non sum dignus*, expressions of repentance and humility accompanying the breaking of the bread and the call of the faithful to communion.

As noted in the Reply no. 2 of the comments in Not 14 (1978) 301, when the rubrics of the Missal of Paul VI say nothing, it is not to be thereby inferred that the former rubrics must be followed (see no. 51 above). The reformed Missal does not supplement but supplants the former Missal. The old Missal at the *Agnus Dei* had the directive "striking his breast three times" and the same for the *Domine, non sum dignus*. But because the new Missal says nothing on this point (*Ordo Missae*, nos. 131 and 133), there is no reason for requiring any gesture to be added to these invocations: Not 14 (1978) 534-535, no. 10.

89.   QUERY: Before the biblical readings sometimes priests or lay readers announce subtitles for the selection or even the rubric: "The first reading," "The second reading," etc. Is it permissible to follow this practice? **REPLY:** Clearly not. As with all rubrics, the titles, "The first reading," "The second reading," are guides for the convenience of the reader. As to the captions, which consist either in a sentence drawn from the text or in a summary statement of the reading, they too are guides useful for choosing among different texts, especially in the Commons. The sole title to be announced is the one indicating the book of the Bible or, where applicable, its author. For example: "A reading from the Letter of Paul to Timothy"; "A reading from the holy Gospel according to Mark": Not 14 (1978) 303, no. 5.

97.   QUERY: In the celebration of Mass may the bishop give the homily at the chair and seated? **REPLY:** By rule of the GIRM no. 97, in the celebration of Mass the homily is given at the chair or at the lectern. In keeping with custom, the bishop may certainly give the homily seated: Not 10 (1974) 80, no. 3. See also no. 42 above.

101.   QUERY: At the presentation of gifts at a Mass with congregation, persons (lay or religious) bring to the altar the bread and wine which are to be consecrated. These gifts are received by the priest celebrant. All those participating in the Mass accompany this group procession in which the gifts are brought forward. They then stand around the altar until communion time. Is this procedure in conformity with the spirit of the law and of the Roman Missal? **REPLY:** Assuredly, the Eucharistic celebration is the act of the entire community, carried out by all the members of the liturgical assembly. Nevertheless, everyone must have and also must observe his or her own place and proper role: "In liturgical celebrations each one, minister or layperson, who has an office to perform, should do all of, but only, those parts which pertain to that office by the nature of the rite and the principles of liturgy." (SC art. 29).

During the liturgy of the eucharist, only the presiding celebrant remains at the altar. The assembly of the faithful take their place in the Church outside the *presbyterium*, which is reserved for the celebrant or concelebrants and altar ministers: Not 17 (1981) 61.

102. QUERY: How are the presentation of the bread and wine by the faithful and the presentation of the paten with the bread in GIRM no. 102 compatible? **REPLY:** There is no problem. For the offerings that the priest receives from the people are put on a nearby table and the bread and wine are carried to the altar (see GIRM no. 101), then the offertory rites take place. If the celebrant takes the paten or ciborium with the bread from the faithful last, he may proceed directly to the altar and immediately recite the formulary for offering the bread: Not 6 (1970) 404, no. 43.

105. See no. 51 above.

108. QUERY: Some celebrants have the practice of raising then joining their hands during the dialogue before the preface and at the beginning of the final blessing. Others omit such gestures. What is right? **REPLY:** As is often the case, at issue is a habit having its source in the rubrics of the former Roman Missal. The current directives of the Order of Mass are to be followed, which are clear on the two points raised: a. As to the dialogue before the preface, no. 27 (MR p. 392) says precisely: "With hands extended he sings or says: *The Lord be with you;*" "He lifts up his hands and continues: *Lift up your hearts;*" "With hands extended, he continues: *Let us give thanks to the Lord our God;*" "The priest continues the preface with hands extended." Therefore, the former rite is not to be continued; among other things it indicated at this point: "He joins his hands before his breast and bows his head as he says: *Let us give thanks. . . .*" b. As to the blessing at the end of Mass, the new Order of Mass says only: "The priest blesses the people, with these words . . ."(no. 42). But the rubrics of the former Order of Mass, after the dismissal *Ite, Missa est*, prescribed a gesture for the blessing having five steps: "Raising his eyes, extending, raising, and joining his hands, and bowing his head to the cross, he says: *May almighty God bless you. . .*and turning to the people. . .continues: *the Father. . .*" Now, however, only that gesture is required which is indicated by the revelant rubric, namely, the priest blesses the people, with the words: *May almighty God bless you, the Father, and the Son, and the Holy Spirit:* Not 14 (1978) 536-537, no. 12.

109 QUERY: Is a bell to be rung at Mass? **REPLY:** It all depends on the different circumstances of places and people, as is clear from GIRM no. 109: "A little before the consecration, the server may ring a bell as a signal to the faithful. Depending on local custom, he also rings the bell at the showing of both the host and the chalice." From a long and attentive catechesis and education in liturgy, a particular liturgical assembly may be able to take part in the Mass with such attention and awareness that it has no need of this signal at the central part of the Mass. This may easily be the case, for example, with religious communities or with particular or small groups. The opposite may be presumed in a parish or public church, where there is a different level of liturgical and religious education and where often people who are visitors or are not regular churchgoers take part. In these cases the bell as a signal is entirely appropriate and is sometimes necessary. To conclude: usually a signal with the bell should be given, at least at the two elevations, in order to elicit joy and attention: Not 8 (1972) 343.

112. QUERY 1: In churches without an altar facing the people should the priest in the celebration of Mass turn toward the congregation as he says: *The peace of the Lord be with you always* and *Let us offer each other a sign of peace?* **REPLY:** Yes. The rubric in the Order of Mass with a congregation no. 128 directs that the priest speaks these words while facing the congregation: Not 6 (1970) 264, no. 39.

QUERY 2: In some places there is a current practice whereby those taking part in the Mass replace the giving of the sign of peace at the deacon's invitation by holding hands during the singing of the Lord's Prayer. Is this acceptable? **REPLY:** The prolonged holding of hands is of itself a sign of communion rather than of peace. Further, it is a liturgical gesture introduced spontaneously but on personal initiative; it is not in the rubrics. Nor is there any clear explanation of why the sign of peace at the invitation: *Let us offer each other the sign of peace* should be supplanted in order to bring a different gesture with less meaning into another part of the Mass: the sign of peace is filled with meaning, graciousness, and Christian inspiration. Any substitution for it must be repudiated: Not 11 (1975) 226.

113. See no. 56e above.

114. QUERY: After the commingling and during the prayer, *Lord, Jesus Christ, Son of the living God* or *Lord Jesus Christ, with faith*, some celebrants place their joined hands on the altar and, with bowed head, say the text of the prayer softly. Is this procedure still to be followed? **REPLY:** Traces of the former rites are here again discernible. To resolve this query the norms of the Order of Mass have to be heeded, with care not to add anything and with attention once again to the principle so kindly stated by Pope John XXIII: "Make complex and difficult matters simple; what is already simple leave alone." The former *Ritus servandus* regarding this prayer directed (no. X, 3): "Then with joined hands placed on the altar, eyes fixed on the sacrament, and bowing over he says softly. . ." The Order of Mass of Paul VI (no. 132) more precisely determines what the GIRM says in no. 114: "Then the priest, with hands joined, says softly. . ." Therefore, the celebrant stands upright with hands joined before his breast: Not 14 (1978) 537-538, no. 13.

115. See no. 87 above.

121. See no. 21 above.

124. QUERY 1: When at the end of Mass one of the solemn blessings or the prayer over the people is used, how is it to be integrated into the concluding rite? **REPLY:** The GIRM no. 124 indicates that on certain days and occasions another, more solemn form of blessing or the prayer over the people precedes this form of blessing as the rubrics direct. The rite in this case takes the following form. After the greeting, *The Lord be with you,* the deacon or the priest himself, if there is no deacon, says the invitation, *Bow your heads and pray for God's blessing* or something similar. Then the priest, with hands outstretched over the people, says the solemn blessing or the prayer over the people, then the words of the blessing; all reply: *Amen* (see MR 495 and 507): Not 6 (1970) 404, no. 41.

QUERY 2: The use of the solemn blessings and prayers over the people that are in the Roman Missal (MR, *ed. typica altera*, 1975, 495-511) expand and add solemnity to the conclusion of the Mass. This form of the concluding rite grows in use as the texts are translated and inserted into the missal proper to each region. But practice varies: a. The celebrant omits the greeting, *The Lord be with you,* before the blessing. b. The deacon or the celebrant omits the invitation, *Bow your heads and ask for God's blessing,* given in the Missal (MR 495 and 507). c. The priest omits extending his hands over the congregation (MR 495 and 507). d. At the blessing the priest sometimes uses the form, *May almighty God bless you. . .,* sometimes, *May the blessing of almighty God. . . .* **REPLY:** In this case also the queries arising from such diversity can be answered from a careful reading of the Roman Missal: a. The rubrics of the Missal (GIRM no. 124; Order of Mass no. 142) expressly lay down the steps in the conclusion of the celebration: first the greeting ("the priest. . .greets the people"), then the blessing ("he continues. . .blessing"), then the dismissal ("he adds immediately"). Furthermore, one of the solemn blessings or prayers over the people may be substituted for the usual formula for the blessing, *May almighty God bless you,* which follows the greeting of the celebrant. Clearly these formularies have the same status as the text of the usual blessing. Therefore, the celebrant's greeting,

The Lord be with you, must precede them. b. The rubric at the beginning of this part of the Missal says: ". . .may give the invitation: *Bow your heads and pray for God's blessing*" (MR 495 and 507). Therefore, the deacon or the priest celebrant is at liberty to use this invitation, to put it in different words, or to omit it altogether. c. But in contrast this same rubric also gives an explicit directive: "The priest extends his hands over the congregation while he says or sings the blessing." Therefore, he holds his hands extended over the congregation during the entire blessing and during it the people respond: *Amen* to each part of this blessing. The priest performs the same gesture over the assembly during the prayer over the people. d. The celebrant as a rule uses the formulary: *May almighty God bless you. . .* (MR, *ed. typica altera*, 1975, pp. 495-506): Not 14 (1978) 306-307, no. 9.

153. QUERY: At the eucharist where several bishops concelebrate, is the use of the pastoral staff restricted to the presiding bishop only, even if he is not the Ordinary of the place of celebration? **REPLY:** In all the liturgical rites, use of the pastoral staff belongs only to the principal celebrant of the eucharist or the one who presides over the liturgy and to no other bishops regardless of their rank.

In the rite of ordination of bishops, the newly ordained use(s) the pastoral staff at the conclusion of the celebration, in accordance with the rubrics of the Roman Pontifical: Not 17 (1981) 231.

158d. QUERY: Does the permission granted to religious to celebrate or concelebrate twice when they concelebrate with their own Ordinary apply also in the case of Ordinary's delegate? **REPLY:** Yes, just as this is granted to priests concelebrating with the diocesan bishop or his delegate (see GIRM no. 158d): Not 5 (1969) 403, no. 13.

170. QUERY: In the manner of concelebrating we find the following differences: a. Sometimes the celebrant's voice stands out clearly, while the concelebrants recite the eucharistic prayer in a low or subdued voice. In other cases, conversely, a clash of loud voices is heard, as though each were striving to outdo the others. b. In carrying out the epiclesis before the consecration not all concelebrants stretch out their hands toward the gifts to invoke the action of the Holy Spirit, but they are extremely careful to do so during the consecration. c. During the epiclesis some bring their hands back as soon as the principal concelebrant has made the sign of the cross over the gifts; others keep their hands outstretched until the text of the epiclesis is concluded. Which ways are right? **REPLY:** To decide which of the differences are right, it is enough to consider the nature of the functions that each concelebrant performs and the nature of the corresponding gesture: a. According to the GIRM no. 170 the assembly of the faithful must distinctly hear the voice of the one presiding. This can be achieved by use of a sensitive and well-placed microphone and especially by the modulation of the concelebrants' voices (*submissa voce*). Otherwise, as in the second case cited, the unity of tone and rhythm for the assembly's understanding of the text cannot be achieved. b. It is rather odd that the norms of the Missal envision a situation quite the opposite from the one alleged: during the epiclesis of the consecration all the concelebrants must hold their hands over the gifts (GIRM nos. 174a, 180a, 184a, 188a: "with hands outstretched toward the gifts") in invoking the action of the Holy Spirit. But during the consecration, the concelebrants hold the right hand toward the bread and the chalice, "if this seems appropriate" (GIRM nos. 174c, 180c, 184c, 188c) and they do so as they recite the *words of the Lord*, namely, up to "Do this in memory of me" inclusive. c. The act of holding the hands outstretched must accompany the words of the prayer. This is why the rubrics of the Order of Mass (nos. 90, 103, 110, 119) indicate the end of this action by saying: "He joins his hands": Not 14 (1978) 303-304, no. 6. See also DOL 242.

191. QUERY: It is apparent that practices differ greatly in the recitation or singing of the doxology concluding the eucharistic prayer: a. Sometimes the principal celebrant alone says or sings it. b. Or regularly all the concelebrants say or sing it. c. In some places the whole assembly says or sings it. What rule should be followed? **REPLY:** In any meeting it customarily belongs to the one presiding to open and close the proceedings that are the purpose of the meeting. In the case of the eucharist the essential part of the entire celebration is clearly the eucharistic prayer, which extends from the preface to the final doxology inclusive. Therefore, it belongs to the one presiding to open this prayer with the preface; this is followed by the *Sanctus*, in which the assembly joins, then the one presiding alone recites the *Father, you are holy indeed* (or the parallel text). As to the concluding doxology, the three cases reported call for the following remarks: a. It is the right of the one who presides and who opened the eucharistic prayer also to close it by reciting the final doxology. This is exactly what the GIRM no. 191 indicates: "The concluding doxology of the eucharistic prayer is recited. . .by the principal celebrant alone." b. The second case reflects the prevailing usage, which almost everywhere concelebrants have quickly adopted in reciting or singing this conclusion together. This usage also conforms to the GIRM no. 191, the second part of which refers to it: ". . .or by all the concelebrants together with the principal celebrant." c. Unlike the two preceding cases, the recitation or singing of the conclusion by the whole assembly is an extension that is unlawful not merely from a disciplinary point of view—as being against the rules now in force—but at a deeper level, namely, as being in conflict with the very nature of ministries and texts.

Even though someone could interpret this extension to the entire assembly as a sign of the desire of the assembly for increased participation in the liturgy, it is necessary that this desire be realized in an orderly and authentic way. What seems like progress is in fact retrogression: it is a sign of forgetting the part that belongs to each individual in the liturgical celebration. See SC art. 28: ". . .each person, minister or layperson, who has an office to perform, should do all, but only those parts which pertain to that office by the nature of the rite and the principles of liturgy." In the third case it happens often that the final *Amen* is said or sung by no one or almost no one. If, on the contrary, the directions given in the Order of Mass (nos. 100, 108, 115, 124, "The people respond: *Amen*") are followed, it is possible in order to give greater emphasis to this response to use more elaborate chants that give force and solemnity to the acclamation of all the people (for example, the triple *Amen* sung by all the people at a Mass celebrated by the pope or the more simple *Amen* in the French missal of 1974, p. 103): Not 14 (1978) 304-305, no. 7.

223. QUERY: When there is no member of the faithful present able to make the acclamation after the consecration, should the priest say: *Let us proclaim the mystery of faith?* **REPLY:** No. The words *the mystery of faith*, which have been removed from the context of Christ's own words and put after the consecration, "serve as an introduction to the acclamation" (Ap. Const. *Missale Romanum*). But when no member of the faithful is present who is able to respond to the acclamation, the priest omits saying: *Let us proclaim the mystery of faith.* The case is like that of a Mass which, because of serious need, is celebrated without any server and, therefore, without the greetings and the blessings at the end of Mass (GIRM no. 211). The same reply applies to a concelebration by priests at which no member of the faithful is present: Not 5 (1969) 324-325, no. 3.

229. See no. 238 below.

234b. QUERY: Some of the acts of reverence by both the celebrant and the people have fallen into disuse, for example, the profound bow to be made in place of the former genuflection at the words announcing the mystery of the incarnation in the *Credo*. Are such gestures still to be observed? **REPLY:** Clearly people should express their faith, devotion, and reverence not only by words but also by gestures and posture. All the more care should be taken about this because the gestures now prescribed since the reform of the liturgy are fewer and simpler. Thus the Order of Mass and the GIRM assign a few instances when gestures are to accompany the words. It is enough to recall the GIRM no. 234 to recognize these various cases: "A bow of the head is made when the three divine persons are named together and at the name of Jesus, Mary, and the saint in whose honor Mass is celebrated. A bow of the body, or profound bow, is made: toward the altar if there is no tabernacle with the blessed sacrament; during the prayers, *Almighty God, cleanse* and *Lord God, we ask you to receive*; within the profession of faith at the words, *by the power of the Holy Spirit*; in Eucharistic Prayer I (Roman Canon) at the words, *Almighty God, we pray*." In the case of the words in the *Credo* the rubric of the Order of Mass also reads: "All bow." It is well to remember that at the Mass of the Christmas Vigil, the Mass at Midnight, the Mass at Dawn, and the Mass during the Day, there is genuflection at the words *And* *he became man* (see MR pp. 153, 155, 156, 157); the same holds for Mass on the solemnity of the Annunication of Our Lord (see MR p. 538).

For the consecration of the bread and wine the GIRM no. 234b prescribes: "The priest bends over slightly as he says the words of the Lord at the consecration." Further the priest genuflects "after the showing of the host," and "after the showing of the chalice" (GIRM no. 233); "he genuflects in adoration" (Order of Mass, nos. 91-92, 104-105, 111-112, 120-121). As for concelebrants, they stand at the showing of the host and chalice, look at them, then bow profoundly (GIRM nos. 174c, 180c, 184c, 188c).

Likewise before communion there are gestures of reverence and faith made by both the celebrant and the people who receive communion. For the celebrant the GIRM no. 115 and the Order of Mass no. 133 have ". . .then the priest genuflects, takes the host" etc.; and for concelebrants the GIRM directs: "One by one the concelebrants come to the middle of the altar, genuflect, and reverently take the body of Christ from the altar. Then holding the eucharistic bread in the right hand, with the left hand under it, they return to their places. The concelebrants may, however, remain in their places and take the body of Christ from the paten presented to them by the principal celebrant or by one or more of the concelebrants, or from the paten as it is passed from one to the other" (GIRM no. 197). As for the people, when they receive the eucharist standing, they are able to make some sign of reverence (GIRM nos. 244c, 245b, 246b, 247b): Not 14 (1978) 535-536, no. 11.

237. QUERY: The GIRM no. 237 says that particles of the eucharistic bread are to be collected after the consecration, but it is not clear what is to be done about them. **REPLY:** The GIRM no. 237 must be taken in context with other articles that deal with the same point. The description of the basic form of celebration says clearly: "After communion the priest returns to the altar and collects any remaining particles. Then, standing at the side of the altar or at the side table, he purifies the paten or ciborium *over the chalice*, then purifies the chalice . . . and dries it with a purificator" (GIRM no. 120). The Order of Mass with a congregation no. 138 says: "After communion the priest or deacon purifies the paten *over the chalice* and the chalice itself." The Order of Mass without a congregation no. 31 says: "Then the priest purifies the chalice *over the paten* and the chalice itself." The point, therefore, is quite clear: Not 8 (1972) 195.

238. QUERY: After the distribution of communion the priest often is observed purifying the vessels (chalice, paten, ciborium) at the middle of the altar. Cannot a better place and time be chosen to do this? May another minister purify the vessels? **REPLY:** a. The directives in the GIRM are to be observed. There is a general principle in no. 238: "The vessels are purified by the priest or else by the deacon or acolyte after the communion or after Mass, if possible at a side table." The directive as to time (whether after communion or after Mass) is completed in no. 229 with one regarding place (at the side of the altar). It is implicit in this regulation that the celebrant never stands at the middle of the altar as he purifies the vessels (see also no. 120). b. Other particulars are found elsewhere in the GIRM: As the priest, no. 120: "After communion the priest returns to the altar and collects any remaining particles. Then, standing at the side of the altar or at a side table, he purifies the paten or ciborium over the chalice, then purifies the chalice, saying quietly: *Lord, may I receive these gifts,* etc., and dries it with a purificator. If this is done at the altar, the vessels are taken to a side table by a minister. It is also permitted, especially if there are several vessels to be purified, to leave them, properly covered and on a corporal, either at the altar or at a side table and to purify them after Mass when the people have left."

As to the deacon, no. 138: "After communion, the deacon returns to the altar with the priest and collects any remaining fragments. He then takes the chalice and other vessels to the side table, where he purifies them and arranges them in the usual way; the priest returns to the chair. But it is permissible to leave the vessels to be purified, properly covered and on a corporal, at a side table and to purify them after Mass, when the people have left."

As to the acolyte, no. 147: "After communion, the acolyte helps the priest or deacon to purify and arrange the vessels. If no deacon is present, the acolyte takes the vessels to the side table, where he purifies and arranges them."

The remarks on the priest, deacon and acolyte are applicable to a special minister who lawfully distributes communion (see SCDS, Instr. *Immensae caritatis;* RR, *Holy Communion and Worship of the Eucharist outside Mass,* no. 17). See also GIRM no. 229 on a priest celebrating without a congregation; nos. 202-206 on a concelebrated Mass: Not 14 (1978) 593-594, no. 15.

257. See no. 272 below.

263. QUERY: Should an altar with a table of wood or metal be consecrated? **REPLY:** Yes, The GIRM no. 263 says: "According to the Church's traditional practice and the altar's symbolism, the table of a fixed altar should be of stone and indeed of natural stone. But at the discretion of the conference of bishops some other solid, becoming, and well-crafted material may be used." The consecration should be carried out according to the existing practice until a new rite is ready: Not 6 (1970) 263, no. 34.

265. QUERY: Has the formulary for the blessing of a movable altar been completed and where is it available? **REPLY:** According to the GIRM no. 265, movable altars may only be blessed. The blessing formulary has not yet been completed: Not 6 (1970) 263, no. 35. (Subsequent to this response, the Congregation of Sacraments and Divine Worship published the rite of Dedication of a Church and an Altar, May 29, 1977.)

269. QUERY: Must the lighted candles that are to be placed in candlesticks for the celebration of Mass consist in part of beeswax, olive oil, or other vegetable oil? **REPLY:** The GIRM prescribes candles for Mass "as a sign of reverence and festiveness" (nos. 79, 269). But it makes no further determination regarding the material of their composition, except in the case of the sanctuary lamp, the fuel for which must be oil or wax (see *Holy Communion and Worship of the Eucharist outside Mass*, Introduction no. 11). The faculty that the conferences of bishops possess to choose suitable materials for sacred furnishings applies, therefore, to the candles for Mass. That faculty is limited only by the condition that in the estimation of the people the materials are valued and worthy and that they are appropriate for sacred use. Candles intended for liturgical use should be made of material that can provide a living flame without being smoky or noxious and that does not stain the altar cloths or coverings. Electric bulbs are banned in the interest of safeguarding authenticity and the full symbolism of light: Not 10 (1974) 80, no. 4.

272. QUERY: When there is no celebrant's chair and no special place for carrying out the liturgy of the word, may a priest who celebrates with a small group present: a. remain at the altar during the liturgy of the word? b. set the missal on the right side of the altar or at the middle? c. and if so, which side of the altar is designated as the left or right? **REPLY:** a. The liturgical norms in force make a clear distinction between the altar and the place for proclaiming the word of God (GIRM nos. 252-257). Where places have not yet been remodeled in keeping with the reformed liturgy (and such remodeling should be done without delay), it is necessary to provide at least a chair for the celebrant and a movable lectern for the reader. When the celebrant himself must act as reader, especially for the gospel, the reading should be at the movable lectern. In the very exceptional case when not even a bench can be set up, the priest may stay at the altar, where the missal and lectionary are set on a reading stand. b. This stand obviously should be placed conveniently for the celebrant's reading, for example, at the middle of the altar. The custom of setting the missal stand on the left side of the altar comes from the time when the chalice was placed at the center at the beginning of Mass. This is no longer the case, since reform of the liturgy, because the chalice is now placed on a side table, away from the altar. c. The left side of the altar is the side at the celebrant's left; the right side, at his right. Not 14 (1978) 302, no. 3.

273. See no. 21, Query 3, above.

283. QUERY: In the GIRM no. 283 what does *eucharistic bread* mean? **REPLY:** The term means the same thing as the *host* hitherto in use, except that the bread is larger in size. The term *eucharistic bread* in line 2 is explained by the words of line 4: "The priest is able actually *to break the host into parts.*" Thus line 2 is about this eucharistic element as to its *kind* and line 4 as to its *shape.* Therefore, it was incorrect to interpret *eucharistic bread* in line 2 as a reference to its shape as though the term implies that bread in the shape designed for its everyday use may be substituted for the host in its traditional shape. The GIRM in no way intended to change the shape of the large and small hosts, but only to provide an option regarding size, thickness, and color in order that the host may really have the appearance of bread that is shared by many people: Not 6 (1970) 37, no. 24.

284. Card. F. Seper, Prefect of the SCDF addressed the following letter, May 2, 1974, Prot. No. 88/74, to Card. J. Krol, President of the Conference of Bishops of the United States:

For some time different Ordinaries have asked this Sacred Congregation for the permission to allow priests who are undergoing a treatment for alcoholism or who have undergone this treatment, to celebrate Mass with unfermented grape juice.

With this situation in mind, the Congregation for the Doctrine of the Faith authorizes the Ordinaries of the United States of America to grant to those priests who have made this request the permission either to concelebrate with one or more priests a normal Mass but without receiving communion under the species of wine or, when this is not possible, to celebrate Mass using unfermented grape juice and to use water alone for the ritual ablutions after Communion. Also, one must avoid creating scandal for the faithful.

In the hope of meeting the concern shown by the bishops for those of their priests suffering from alcoholism and in asking you to inform the Ordinaries of the permission that is granted to them, I am sincerely yours.

296. QUERY: In consecrating vessels not made of gold should the formularies of the Roman Pontifical be used? **REPLY:** Yes. Whatever the material of their composition, provided this is solid and noble in the judgment of the conference of bishops, vessels are to be blessed or consecrated according to the rites appearing in the liturgical books (see GIRM no. 296). The formularies to be used remain those from the Roman Pontifical, with an anointing added in the case of consecration: Not 6 (1970) 263, no. 36.

299. QUERY: May the priest omit wearing the stole? **REPLY:** No. The query arises from an interpretation of the GIRM no. 299. The contents of that number, "The chasuble is the vestment proper to the priest celebrant, at Masses and other rites. . .," must be understood as governed by nos. 81 and 302. From these it is altogether clear that the stole is a priestly vestment that never is to be left off at Mass and other rites directly connected with Mass: Not 6 (1970) 104, no. 30.

308b. QUERY: On Passion Sunday is the color red worn only in the palms procession? **REPLY:** No. Red is the color for the Mass and office for the entire liturgical day on Passion, that is, Palm Sunday, namely, from Evening Prayer I to Evening Prayer II. The same applies to Good Friday, on which red is the color for both the office and the Celebration of the Lord's Passion: Not 5 (1969) 403, no. 12.

316. QUERY: May Masses for various needs and occasions and votive Masses be celebrated on weekdays of the Christmas and Easter seasons? **REPLY:** The GIRM no. 316(c) speaks only of the weekdays in Ordinary Time and not of the weekdays of the Christmas and Easter seasons. But a comparison of the GIRM with the General Norms for the Liturgical Year and the Calendar leads to the following interpretation. 1. Masses for various needs and occasions or votive Masses are forbidden on solemnities, the Sundays of Advent, Lent, and the Easter season, as well as on Ash Wednesday and the weekdays of Holy Week, which "have precedence over all other celebrations" (see GNLYC no. 16). 2. On the Sundays other than those just listed, on feasts, on the weekdays of Advent from 17 to 24 December and of Lent, such Masses may be said "in cases of serious need, at the direction of the local Ordinary or with his permission" (GIRM no. 332). 3. On the weekdays of Advent, up to December 16 inclusive, during the Christmas season from January 2 to the Saturday after Epiphany, during the Easter season from the Tuesday after the octave of Easter until the Saturday before Pentecost, and on obligatory memorials, "if some real need or pastoral advantage requires, at the discretion of the rector of the church or the priest celebrant, the Masses corresponding to such need or advantage may be used in a celebration with a congregation" (GIRM no. 333). The need in question is to be understood in a pastoral sense, for example, if a large number of people gathers for a particular celebration, as is the case in some places on the first Friday of the month. Apart from such situations Masses for various needs and occasions are not allowed. During these seasons the weekday office has a certain priority in order that the mystery of salvation, rather than other feasts or commemorations, may be celebrated in the measure due to it (see SC art. 108). This applies above all to the fifty days from Easter Sunday to Pentecost, days that are celebrated "as one feast day, or better as 'one great Sunday' " (GNLYC no. 22). 4. During Ordinary Time it is permissible to celebrate any of the Masses for various needs and occasions whenever the office is of the weekday or an optional memorial occurs. 5. Masses for the dead are regulated in the same way. a. The Mass of burial may be celebrated on any day, except the Easter triduum, the Sundays of Advent, Lent, and Easter, and solemnities. b. The Masses on the occasions of news of a death, final burial, and the first anniversary may be celebrated on the days indicated in nos. 3-4 (see GIRM no. 337). c. Daily Masses for the dead may be celebrated on the weekdays in Ordinary Time and when an optional memorial occurs, as in no. 4: Not 5 (1969) 323-324, no. 2.

316c. QUERY: On weekdays in Ordinary Time may the Mass of any saint one chooses be celebrated? **REPLY:** Yes. The GIRM no. 316c says: "On the weekdays in Ordinary Time, the priest may choose the weekday Mass, the Mass of an optional memorial, the Mass of a saint inscribed in the martyrology for that day, a Mass for various needs and occasions, or a votive Mass." The votive Masses listed are those "of the mysteries of the Lord or in honor of Mary or of a particular saint or of all the saints" (GIRM no. 329c).

Even though no. 316c gives a certain precedence to those saints mentioned in the martyrology for the day, no. 329c at the end allows, as an option in favor of the faithful's devotion, a votive Mass of any saint or all the saints. Texts for votive Masses to be celebrated in honor of the saints are to be chosen in keeping with no. 4, p. 514 of the *Missale Romanum* (RM: Proper of the Saints, Introduction no. 4): Not 10 (1974) 145, no. 2.

322a. QUERY: Are the formularies of the Roman Canon proper to the day still to be followed on Holy Thursday? **REPLY:** Yes. They are not in the new Order of Mass because they are given in their proper place, that is, in the Roman Missal for the Mass of the Lord's Supper on Holy Thursday: Not 5 (1969) 403-404, no. 15.

322c. QUERY: When may the special formulary for the dead be used in Eucharistic Prayers II and III? **REPLY:** The source of this query is the phrasing of the rubric for Eucharistic Prayer III: "When this prayer is used in *Masses for the dead. . .*" (See *Preces eucharisticae et praefationes*, Vatican Polyglot Press, 1967, p. 35). This rubric has been clarified in the new Order of Mass (GIRM no. 322b): "When Mass is celebrated *for any dead person. . .*" Thus the special embolism for the deceased may be used in any Mass that is celebrated for a dead person or in which a dead person receives special remembrance. The purpose of the law is to facilitate the carrying out of the GIRM no. 316 on restraint in using the Masses for the dead: Not 5 (1969) 325, no. 4.

322d. QUERY: When is a particular preface to be regarded as proper? **REPLY:** The problem arises mainly from the possibility of using Eucharistic Prayer IV, which has a fixed preface and consequently is governed by the rule that it may not be used when a Mass has its own proper preface (GIRM no. 322d). Further, the preface of the season is said on feasts and also during the particular seasons, some of which are quite long, and this raises the question of the meaning of "proper preface." A preface is to be regarded as "proper" in a strict sense in Masses that are celebrated on the very day of a feast or during its *octave*. In the Proper of Seasons there is a corresponding preface, but this is not to be regarded as proper strictly speaking and during the season Eucharistic Prayer IV and Eucharistic Prayer II with their own prefaces may be used. In votive Masses there is the option to use either the preface corresponding to the Mass or the preface of any eucharistic prayer: Not 5 (1969) 323, no. 1.

323. QUERY: In Masses on a memorial may the prayer over the gifts and the prayer after communion, unless they are proper, also be taken from the votive Masses or from the votive prayers for various needs and occasions? **REPLY:** The GIRM no. 323 says: "In Masses on a memorial, however. . .the prayer over the gifts and the prayer after communion, unless they are proper, may be taken *either* from the common *or* from the weekday of the current season." For the celebration of a memorial is combined with the celebration of the current weekday; but Masses of saints cannot be combined with the Masses for various needs and occasions: Not 7 (1971) 112, no. 1.

333. QUERY 1: May the votive Masses of Jesus Christ the High Priest, the Sacred Heart, the Immaculate Heart of Mary be celebrated, respectively, on the first Thursday, Friday and Saturday of the month even if an obligatory memorial occurs? **REPLY:** They may be celebrated observing the rule of GIRM no. 333: "If some real need or pastoral advantage requires, at the discretion of the rector of the Church or the priest celebrant, the Masses corresponding to such need or advantage may be used in a celebration with a congregation." The decision about a real need is based on consideration of the sensibilities and devotion of the people: Not 5 (1969) 404, no. 17.

QUERY 2: What is meant by the weekdays of Advent, Christmas, and the Easter season on which "if some real need or pastoral advantage requires, at the discretion of the rector of the Church or the priest celebrant, the Masses corresponding to such need or advantage may be used in a celebration with a congregation" (GIRM no. 333)? **REPLY:** These are the weekdays that are listed in the Table of Liturgical Days no. 13, i.e., "weekdays of Advent up to December 16 inclusive; weekdays of the Christmas season from January 2 until the Saturday after Epiphany; weekdays of the Easter season from the Monday after the octave of Easter until the Saturday before Pentecost inclusive." Since the GIRM no. 333 does not speak of the weekdays of Lent, neither does it intend to speak of the weekdays of Advent from December 17 to 24 inclusive nor of the days within the octave of Christmas, which in the Table of Liturgical Days no. 9 are ranked with the weekdays of Lent: Not 10 (1974) 145, no. 1.

336. QUERY 1: May a funeral Mass be celebrated during the octaves of Christmas and Easter? **REPLY:** Yes. The rule of the GIRM no. 336 is that of the Masses for the dead the one for a funeral may be celebrated on any day except holy days of obligation, the Sundays of Advent and Lent, and Easter Sunday. Therefore, it may be celebrated during the octaves of Christmas or Easter: Not 6 (1970) 263, no. 37.

QUERY 2: May a funeral Mass be celebrated on Holy Thursday and during the Easter triduum? **REPLY:** No. The directives in the Roman Missal apply. On Holy Thursday morning as a rule the chrism Mass is celebrated (MR pp. 239-242). In addition to the evening Mass of the Lord's Supper "the local Ordinary may permit another Mass to be celebrated in churches and public or semipublic oratories in the evening or, in the case of genuine necessity, even in the morning, but exclusively for those who cannot in any way take part in the evening Mass" (MR p. 243 [RM, Holy Thursday "Evening Mass of the Lord's Supper"]). Other eucharistic celebrations on Holy Thursday are entirely forbidden. On Good Friday "according to the Church's ancient tradition, the sacraments are not celebrated" (MR p. 250 [RM, Good Friday,

"Celebration of the Lord's Passion"]). "On Holy Saturday the Church waits at the Lord's tomb,. . .and the sacrifice of the Mass is not celebrated" (MR p. 265 [RM, Holy Saturday]). In the case of Easter Sunday, the GIRM no. 336 already forbids a funeral Mass, since this is a solemnity that is of obligation: Not 10 (1974) 145-146, no. 3.

337. QUERY 1: May the Masses for the dead referred to in the GIRM no. 337 be celebrated even on weekdays of Lent? **REPLY:** Yes. The Masses mentioned in no. 337 (on the occasions of news of a death, final burial, or the first anniversary) may be celebrated *all* weekdays, with the exception only of Ash Wednesday and the weekdays of Holy Week: Not 6 (1970) 264, no. 38.

QUERY 2: May a Mass for the dead after news of a death or on the day of final burial or the first anniversary be celebrated even within the octave of Christmas? **REPLY:** Yes. According to the GIRM no. 337 these Masses are allowed on weekdays from December 17 to 24 inclusive and on the weekdays of Lent. Therefore, they may be celebrated on days within the octave of Christmas, which the Table of Liturgical Days no. 9 ranks with those weekdays: Not 10 (1974) 146, no. 4.